# Wines & Beers of Old New England

Sanborn C. Brown

# Wines & Beers o

## A How-to-do-it History

DRAWINGS BY ED LINDLOF

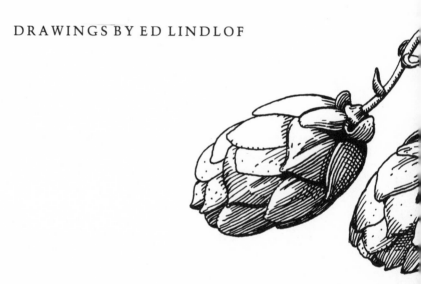

THE UNIVERSITY PRESS OF NEW ENGLAND

# Old New England

HANOVER, NEW HAMPSHIRE 1978

Copyright © 1978 by Trustees of Dartmouth College
All Rights Reserved
Library of Congress Catalogue Card Number 77-72519
International Standard Book Number 0-87451-144-5 (cloth)
International Standard Book Number 0-87451-148-8 (paper)
Printed in the United States of America
Designed by Richard Hendel

The University Press
of New England

*Sponsoring Institutions*

# Contents

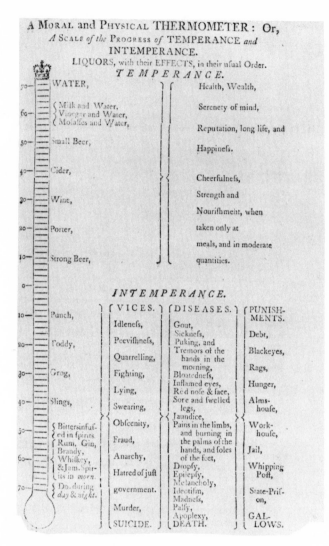

Dr. Benjamin Rush's Moral and Physical Thermometer from
*The Medical And Agricultural Register*, Volume 1, Number 11,
November 1806.

# Preface

This book is written for people who like to go to folk museums, who like to collect antiques, who like to renovate old houses, and who like to drink. There are abundant records of how our New England ancestors quenched their thirst, much of it in the form of old grandfather's tales, and some of it accurate enough so that if you really want to collect an old-fashioned beverage museum for yourself, it is both satisfying and fun.

Taste and smell are difficult to describe by the written or spoken word. To understand what the colonial Americans meant when they talked of small beer, applejack, or metheglin, it is not enough to describe what the beverages were and why they developed; you must actually drink, taste, and smell. That creates a problem. Few of us live in woods where we can chop down a forty-foot-high black birch tree whenever we want to make five gallons of birch beer, and even fewer have the readily available free labor of large families with many children brought up in a culture where they are expected to work for one another day and night. Yet to make five gallons of birch beer requires that every leaf bud be gathered from the forty-foot tree as flavoring for the finished drink as it was made in the eighteenth century. To reconcile the necessity of tasting with the impracticality of trying to recreate every old technique and method, I have carried on the investigation in double fashion. Once having successfully mastered the art of any particular drink, I have used the end product as a norm against which to test more practical recipes for our modern living. The book follows this procedure by including both the old and the new.

My aim is to describe and make real the history of the technology of wine and beer making in the New England frontier. This book differs markedly from the many volumes devoted to home wine and beer making. In general, those who find pleasure in making home-fermented drinks try to create equivalents to accepted types and tastes. Books and magazines abound to tell the enthusiast how to make beers and ales; yeasts are readily available to simulate clarets, burgundies, madeiras or champagnes; and success is gauged by how indistinguishable the home product is from the "genuine." This is very far from the idea of recreating an ancient taste. In terms of looks, a lovingly brewed lager, fermented with imported yeasts and clarified to a sparkling transparency, rivals in the eyes of the hobbyist the finest on today's market, but it is a far cry from the murky, muddy-looking porter that was so highly praised by the first president of the United States.

Only a tiny fraction of the farmers who brewed and fermented their beverages ever wrote down or recorded what they did, and much of what we know has therefore come down to us by notably unreliable oral history. No family recipes and techniques that old men say their grandfathers or their grandmothers used can be taken at face value. Nevertheless, by listening carefully to what is said and then transforming these comments into experimental practice, the technology can be recreated with considerable validity, and though many of the boasts of alcoholic potency or superb bouquet do not survive a scientific reconstruction of tastes and smells, we are probably much nearer the true state of the art as a result of this type of research. You will discover as you read these pages that they constitute a leisurely reconstruction of the past.

To age wine takes a long time, and often years must go by before you can discover whether a given idea is valid. It also takes lots of space, since even if you are experimenting with only ten or twenty gallons a year, a five-year ageing process requires suitable storage for a hundred or so gallons. These two factors alone probably account for why so few people try to reconstruct this fascinating facet of our New England heritage.

One further motivation stimulated the writing of this volume. As our modern society has become more and more complicated, as population continues to increase and our cities become more crowded, a greater and greater number of young people are looking for a simpler, more unhurried, and closer-to-nature way of life. But many who know little about living in the fields and the forests discover their attempts to escape unbearably hard and finally do not make it, not for a lack of will but for a lack of a way. Those who know how to find gourmet salads and vegetables on the roadsides, who can guide the uninitiated to succulent mushrooms on the forest floor, or who know how to provide excellent wine and thirst-satisfying beers from the woods and farmlands have much to offer these fugitives from our overly complex society. For them I have tried to be very specific. I have not assumed that they recognize a sweet birch tree or know the difference between a benign and poisonous sumac. If in the process I have been too detailed for those who already know such things, I offer no apology, for I want this volume in its own limited way to add to the success of those who try to live close to the land.

*Henniker, N.H*                                                    S.C.B.
*March 1977*

# Glossary

This glossary is placed at the beginning of the book in the hope that the reader will thereby be tempted to study it before turning to the text that follows. In a subject as technical as wine and beer making, one expects to find a number of terms that are uniquely specific. Furthermore, this subject was a folk art. Names for all kinds of things were modified from time to time and from place to place, and the meanings of terms changed or disappeared entirely. The glossary is a mixture of modern and ancient terms, the older ones being limited to the New England area.

Since the book is supposed to whet your appetite to do your own delving into the subject, the glossary includes some important terms I have not used. All should help in the understanding of old recipes and techniques that you may uncover for yourself.

One word of warning. Measures like "teaspoon," "tablespoon," "cup," and "dash" are among those which have changed their meanings over the years. You must judge the age of a recipe in order to get the proper proportions of ingredients. Measures are called "old" in this glossary if they were in use before 1800.

ABBOTT'S FLIP a flip with rum and brandy.

ACETIFICATION see *wine, sour.*

ACIDITY used to indicate the quality of tartness or sharpness to the taste.

ACKUBY rum.

AGEING maturing a wine.

AHCOOBEE rum.

AIRLOCK see *waterseal.*

ALAMBIC a goose-neck still.

A L D E H Y D E dehydrogenated alcohol.

A L E B E R R Y ale, wine, oatmeal, and spices.

A L E C O N N E R, A L E - C O N N E R an examiner or inspector of ale or beer.

A L E C O S T ground ivy, used in place of hops.

A L E C U P ale, sherry, ginger beer, and spices.

A L E H O O F ground ivy, used in place of hops.

A L E H O V E ground ivy, used in place of hops.

A L E P O S S E T T ale, cream, eggs, and spices.

A M E L I O R A T I O N adding sugar and/or water to the must.

A M P E L O G R A P H Y the scientific description of a vine.

A N C H O R I C E loose ice crystals of frozen cider.

A N G E L I C A a sweet mixture of wine and brandy.

A P P L E B R A N D Y distillate from crushed fermented apples.

A P P L E J A C K a beverage produced by freezing hard cider.

A P P L E P A L S Y intoxication.

A P P L E W H I S K E Y a blend of apple brandy and cider spirits.

A R G I L clay.

A R O M A the basic scent of a wine. The direct smell of the grapes in wine, which after ageing in the bottle develops into a bouquet.

A U G U S T S W E E T see *sweet bough.*

A U L D M A N ' S M I L K a hot drink with ale, eggs, whiskey, and spices.

B A C K S large vessels of any kind intended to hold wort.

B A G a dry measure; 1 bag = 3 bushels.

B A L A N C E the right proportion of sugar and acidity in wine, yielding a pleasant impression to the taste.

B A L D W I N bright red apple; origin in Wilmington, Mass., about 1780.

B A L K a section of a log from which barrel staves are split.

B E E R : S M A L L or S I N G L E made from only the sugar in the malt. A weak beer.

MIDDLE or SHIPS or TABLE made with some sugar added to the malt. An average beer.

DOUBLE or OLD or STRONG made with enough sugar to assure high alcoholic content.

B E L L O W S - T O P a flip, frothed with beaten eggs.

B E N  D A V I S bright deep red apple; origin in southern states, early 1800's.

B E V E R I G E mulled hard cider.

B I T E astringency from acids.

B I T T E R  B E E R top-fermented draught beer darker in color and higher in bitterness level than pale or light ale.

B L A C K  G I L L I F L O W E R red to dark purple apple; origin in Conn., early 1800's.

B L A C K  J A C K heavy black leather tankard mainly used for drinking beer.

B L A C K - S T R A P a mixture of rum and molasses.

B L U E  P E A R M A I N red apple with blue bloom; origin in early 1800's.

B O D Y the consistency, thickness, or substance of a wine as opposed to the lack of body in a light wine.

B O G U S short for calibogus.

B O L T the radial wedge of a balk.

B O T T L E  S I C K N E S S the formation of acetaldehyde due to aeration during bottling.

B O U Q U E T the aroma of a wine. That part of the fragrance of wine which originates from the ageing of the wine as distinct from the fragrance of the grapes used.

B O W L 3 "old" cups.

BRAGOT beer made with malt and honey.

BRANDY, MARC distilled from the marc (pomace), diluted with water after the must has been pressed out. Used almost entirely for fortification.

BRIDAL, BRIDE-ALE, BRIDALE an ale-drinking wedding feast.

BRIX a scale measuring the density or concentration of sugar in solution.

BUNG the wooden plug of the filling hole in a barrel.

BUNG HOLE the hole in the side or end of a barrel.

BUNG STARTER a flat-headed wooden mallet with a long flexible handle for knocking out bungs.

BUSH a maple orchard.

BUSHEL a dry measure: 1 bu. = 4 pecks
= 32 quarts
= 64 pints.

BUTT a cask of 130 gallons.

CALCAREOUS chalky.

CALIBOGUS a mixture of rum and spruce beer.

CAMBIUM LAYER the active growing part of a tree between the wood and the bark.

CAMBRIDGE ALE CUP a hot drink of ale, sherry, and spices.

CARAMELIZATION oxidation of sugar into caramel. Sometimes refers to the addition of caramel to give color to spirits. Often used synonymously with maderization.

CARBOY a large (5 to 15 gallons) glass or plastic bottle.

CASEIN a protein derived from milk used in the clarification of wine.

CATAWBA purplish-red native American grape, a *Vitis Labrusca* variety.

CAT'S-FOOT ground ivy used in place of hops.

CAULIFLOWER-HEAD the foam on fermenting beer.

CHAI cellar where vats, barrels, and bottles are stored.

CHAPTALISATION the addition of sugar to fermenting wine to increase alcoholic content. Named after Jean Chaptal who suggested the process in the eighteenth century.

CHARACTER the qualities of color, bouquet, and taste associated with a particular type of wine at its best.

CHIME the edge or rim of a cask.

CIDER what we now call hard cider.

CIDER, FRESH apple juice.

CIDER, SWEET unfermented cider.

CIDER, WATER see *ciderkin.*

CIDER OIL applejack.

CIDER ROYAL see *royal cider.*

CIDER SPIRITS distillate from hard cider.

CIDERKIN a drink made from the apple pomace by pouring water over the mash after the cider was pressed out, and repressed.

CLARIFICATION the clarifying of wine with beaten egg whites or other agents.

CLEAN wine free of any "off" taste or foreign smells, one that is palatable, agreeable, and refreshing.

CLONE plant variety produced by asexual means; does not reproduce true by seed.

COLONEL BYRD'S NIGHTCAP a hot drink of strong ale, brandy, and cloves.

COOPER a dealer and maker of barrels.

COOPERAGE wooden casks used for ageing wines.

COPPICE TREES trees with several trunks from one set of roots.

CORK DRIVER a corking machine.

CRACKLING slightly effervescent.

C R A Z E to produce minute cracks in old glass or glaze.

C R U I T S spices and other flavoring added to wine.

C U P dry or liquid measure, 1 cup = ½ pint.
= 16 tablespoons.

The old "cup" was ⅕th less than our present 8-ounce cup.

C U T dilute.

C U V E E the content of a wine vat, or all the wine made at one time and under similar conditions. Sometimes means "pressing."

C Y S E R apple wine made with honey.

D A S H one shake of a shaker.

D E C A N T separate the wanted liquid from the lees.

D E C O C T I O N liquid preparation of spices or herbs by boiling to get the flavor.

D E E P a wine that possesses a bouquet of rich, full, and lasting quality.

D E M I J O H N a corrupted English translation of the French "Dame-Jeanne"; refers to large glass bottles with a capacity varying from one to ten gallons, usually enclosed in wickerwork.

D E S S E R T S P O O N ½ tablespoon, 2 fluid drachms, 2 teaspoons when 4 teaspoons equaled 1 tablespoon.

D I A S T A S E an enzyme in grain barley that converts starch into fermentable sugars.

D O U B L E   M A G N U M a bottle holding 96 oz.

D R A C H M 3 scruples apothecary weight.

Fluid Drachm = ⅛ fluid ounce.

D R A W   D O W N pour back.

D R O P S apples that have fallen naturally off the tree.

D R Y lacking in sugar, the opposite of sweet.

DUCHESS OF OLDENBURG a red striped apple, imported from Russia in the early 1800's

DUMELOW see *Wellington Bloomless*.

EARLY BIRDS a warm drink of ale, sugar, spirits, and spices.

EARLY HARVEST a pale yellow apple of unknown origin before 1800.

EARTHY a mineral or organic taste which comes from the soil or terrain where the fruits are grown.

EGG FLIP a flip with eggs, gin or whisky, and spices.

EIGHT-ROWED FLINT the type of corn used in New England before the introduction of sweet corn around 1800.

ELBULUM elderberry beer.

ENOLOGY a corruption of "genology" from the Greek *oinos* = wine plus logy. The knowledge of wine, or the science and technology of wine making.

ESOPUS SPITZENBURG a bright red apple with yellow dots; origin in Esopus, N.Y., before 1800.

ESSENCE OF LOCK JAW applejack.

ESTER an often fragrant compound with a fruity aroma formed by the reaction between an acid and an alcohol with the elimination of water.

EXPRESSION forcible separation of liquids from solids by means of pressure.

FALLAWATER a yellow-pinkish apple; origin in Penn., early 1800's.

FAMEUSE a bright red apple imported from France in the 1700's.

FERMENTATION, FOAMING the period of vigorous fermentation during which great quantities of carbon dioxide are generated.

FERMENTATION LOCK waterseal.

FERMENTATION, QUIET later stages of fermentation, when the emission of carbon dioxide is slight.

FERMENTATION, STORMY see *fermentation, foaming.*

FIASCO round-bottom bottle covered with straw.

FIELD BALM ground ivy used in place of hops.

FIFTH a fifth of a gallon, ⅘ of a quart.

FINE a wine of finesse and polish that has developed perfectly.

FINING the clarification of wine by removing from it all impurities with beaten eggs or other agents.

FINISH the aftertaste impression received after swallowing a well-balanced wine.

FIRKIN liquid measure, now 10.8 gallons, formerly 84 gallons.

FIRM wine characterized by a certain astringency or acidity. The opposite of flabby.

FIT warm beer sweetened with molasses and fortified with rum.

FLABBY the opposite of firm. A wine that lacks tannin.

FLAGGING the gasketing between barrelhead boards.

FLINTY a smell reminiscent of struck flint, found in certain austere dry wines from high mineral soil.

FLIP a hot drink of strong beer, sugar, and rum.

FLIP-DOG a loggerhead.

FOLK WINE a wine not made of grapes but of rhubarb, blackberry, dandelion, etc.

FORTIFIED strengthened by adding alcohol.

FOX intoxicate.

FOXY the distinctive spicy fruity taste of native American grapes. The smell and taste of wines made from the *Vitis Labrusca* grapes, widely grown in New England.

FRAGRANT naturally and pleasantly scented.

FRUITY a term that describes the ripe but not necessarily grapy smell of wine. Wines that are not called "fruity" are often called "vinous".

FULL-BODIED a wine that is pleasingly strong in flavor, taste, or bouquet.

GALLON liquid measure: 1 gal. = 4 quarts
= 8 pints
= 32 gills.

GILL liquid measure, 1 gi. = ½ cup.

GILL-OVER-THE-GROUND ground ivy, used in place of hops.

GINGER ginger root ground as needed, not as strong as present-day powdered product. When using old recipes, reduce amount to ¼ quantity given.

GLASSFUL 1 cup.

GLYCERINE a by-product of sugar and alcohol in wine. It gives "body," "fat," "oiliness," or even "greasiness" to a wine, depending on the amount.

GOODS the ground malt in a mash tub.

GRAIN $\frac{1}{7000}$th of a pound avoirdupois, $\frac{1}{5760}$th of a pound apothecary.

GREEN young.

GRIMES GOLDEN golden yellow apple; origin in West Virginia, before 1800.

GRIST grain or mixtures of grain used in mashing.

GRITS cracked corn used to augment barley malt.

GROG a mixture of rum and water.

GROG-FIGHT a drinking party.

GROG-SHOP a public house.

GROGGED, GROGGY intoxicated.

GROUND IVY a common weed used in place of hops in preserving and flavoring beer.

GUILE a brewing vat.

GYLE wort in the process of fermentation.

GYLE TUN a fermentation tub.

HANDFUL 10 drachms avoirdupois.

HARD alcoholic.

HEAPING as much as could be piled in a spoon without falling off.

HEDGE-HOG QUILLS applejack.

HENS EGG a volume measure, 3 or 4 tablespoons.

HIGH TOP SWEET small yellow apple, favorite in early days of Plymouth Colony.

HIPPOCRAS spiced grape wine made with honey, sometimes served hot.

HOGSHEAD modern = 54 gallons
colonial = 63 to 140 gallons.

HOMEBREW homemade beer, suds.

HONEST a wine that presents no foreign odors or tastes.

HONEY BEER hopped mead.

HOPPING adding hops.

HOPPING, DRY adding hops to the finished beer.

HORN OF GUNPOWDER applejack.

HOT CUP warm drink of ale, sugar, sherry, and spices.

HOT SPICED ALE warm ale, eggs, nutmeg, and buttered toast.

HOT TODDY rum, cinnamon, sugar, and piping hot water.

HOTTLE see *loggerhead*.

HUBBARDSTON yellow or greenish apple mottled with red; origin in Hubbardston, Mass., early 1800's.

HYDROMEL mead.

HYDROMETER an instrument used for measuring the specific gravity of liquids.

INDIAN MOLASSES maple syrup.

JEHU'S NECTAR hot ale, gin, and ginger.

JEROBOAM an oversized bottle whose exact content varies from the equivalent of 4 to 6 bottles. Usually 144 oz.

JERSEY LIGHTNING applejack.

JONATHAN brilliant red apple; origin in Woodstock, N.Y., early 1800's.

KILL-DEVIL rum.

KILNING drying germinated barley in malting.

LABRUSCA native North American grape.

LACTIC ACID one of the organic acids found in wine in an average quantity of 0.5 to 0.1 percent. Its taste is less astringent than that of malic acid.

LADY red and yellow apple imported from France before 1600.

LAMB'S WOOL roasted apples, warm ale, and spices.

LAYER branch of a vine, covered with soil to take root while still part of the parent.

LEES the sludge deposited on the bottom of a bottle or barrel.

LEGS the streaks that run down the sides of a glass after the liquor it contains has been swirled.

LIGHT a pleasing, refreshing wine that is usually on the dry side.

LIGHTNING gin.

LIMING the use of birdlime, a sticky substance smeared on twigs used to catch small birds.

LIVELY the characteristic of wines due to appropriate amount of acidity.

LOGGERHEAD a long-handled iron tool terminating in a ball used to heat wines and beers.

LUPULIN the fine yellow resinous powder on the hop cone that gives it its characteristic flavor and odor.

MACERATION extraction of soluble portions of a substance by prolonged soaking in a liquid.

MADERIZATION caramelization, or the oxidation of old wines exposed to heat.

MAGNUM wine bottle equivalent to two ordinary bottles.

MAIDEN'S BLUSH pale lemon yellow apple with crimson cheeks; origin unknown, early 1800's.

MALIC ACID acid found in fruits which determines ripeness. Ripeness increases as the malic acid decreases.

MALOLACTIC the process by which malic acid is replaced by the less astringent lactic acid.

MALTOSE the fermentable sugar produced during malting.

MAPLE MOLASSES maple syrup.

MAPLE-WATER fresh sap from the maple tree.

MARC see *pomace.*

MARRIAGE the process of oxidation, reduction, and esterification to produce and age wine.

MASHING the process of steeping and boiling ground malt in water.

MATURE describes a wine that possesses balanced aged bouquet and is ready for bottling.

MEAD a drink containing fermented honey.

MELLOW a term for a soft wine that is sometimes slightly on the sweet side.

MELOMEL mead fermented with fruit juices such as cider, raspberry juice, blackberry juice, etc.

METHEGLIN spiced mead.

MIMBO mombo without nutmeg.

MOMBO a mixture of rum, sugar, water, and nutmeg.

MOTHER golden yellow and deep red apple; origin in Bolton, Mass., early 1800's.

MOTHER-IN-LAW half old and half bitter ale!

MUDDLER a churning stick.

MULLED hot and spiced.

MURK the dregs of the first fermentation.

MUST grape juice at fermentation. It may also include skins, pits, and stems as well as pulp.

MUSTY ½ ale, ½ lager beer.

MUTE describes a partially fermented wine in which the fermentation process has been halted by introducing brandy while there is considerable sugar in the wine. Used in the preparation of aperitifs.

NEAT undiluted.

NEGUS hot tawney port or sherry, hot water, sugar, nutmeg, and lemon.

NEUTRAL SPIRITS spirits distilled from any material to a proof of 190 or more.

NEW ENGLAND RUM often called *Medford* or *Newburyport*, a dark rum distilled in New England.

NOGGIN a liquid measure, usually 1 gill.

NORTHERN SPY bright red apple; origin in East Bloomfield, N.Y., around 1800's.

NOSE a word used in describing bouquet; a wine that has a good nose always has a pleasant bouquet.

NUTMEG a hard aromatic seed obtained from the fruit of an evergreen tree indigenous to the East Indian islands, much used in early New England mixed drinks. One grated nutmeg = 2¾ tablespoons of ground nutmeg.

NUTTY used to describe the odor and nutlike flavor of appetizer or dessert wines like sherry.

OENOPHILE a lover of the science of wine or winemaking.

OCTOBER BEER strong beer.

ONE-YARD-OF-FLANNEL a flip with beaten eggs.

OUNCE a unit of weight; 1 oz. = ⅟₁₆ pound dry
= 2 tablespoons
= 8 drachms apothecary
= 16 drachms avoirdupois
= ⅟₁₂ pound fluid.

OVARY the hard green core underneath the petals of a flower which must always be avoided in making flower wines.

PALATE in wine tasting, a synonym for taste sensations taken all together.

PECK a dry measure; 1 pk. = 8 quarts
= 16 pints.

PERFUME the quality of bouquet that is developed in the maturing process, as opposed to the aroma of a wine.

PERCOLATION extracting the flavoring from a finely divided powder by passing a liquid through it.

PERRY cider-like beverage made from pears.

PETILLANT slightly effervescent, crackling.

PIMENT, PYMENT melomel, grape wine made from honey.

PINCH 1 drachm avoirdupois, as much as can be taken between the tip of your finger and thumb.

PINT dry or liquid measure; 1 pt. = 2 cups.

PIPE see *butt.*

PITCHING adding yeast to start fermentation.

P O M A C E ground or crushed fruit pulp including skins, seeds, and stalks; marc.

P O R T E R a dark bitter beer, a mixture of beer, ale, and twopenny.

P O R T E R yellow apple marked with red; origin in Sherburne, Mass., about 1800.

P O T T L E one half gallon.

P O U N D a unit of weight; 1 lb. = 16 ounces.

P R I M I N G the process of adding sugar to continue fermentation in a bottle.

P U N C H brought back from the Orient by sailors, derived from the Hindu *"panch"* meaning 5—for spirits, water, spices, fruits, and sugar.

P U N C H E O N a cask with capacity of between 70 and 120 gallons. Today usually 83 U.S. gallons capacity.

P U N T the part of the bottom of the bottle that is pushed up inside.

P Y M E N T *piment.*

Q U A R T a dry or liquid measure; 1 qt. = 2 pints.

R A C K I N G separating the liquid from the sludge. The transferring of wine from one barrel into another. Siphoning.

R A T T L E - S K U L L a mixture of brandy, rum, wine, and porter, flavored with lime peel and nutmeg.

R H O D E I S L A N D G R E E N I N G green apple; origin in Newport, R.I., about 1700.

R I B S T O N yellow or greenish apple imported from Yorkshire, England, about 1700.

R I C H applied to wine that is full-bodied, flavorful, generous, and robust.

R I P E applied to wine that attained full mellowness and perfection and is at its best.

RIVING splitting, as of wood.

ROBE a wine's color.

ROBIN-IN-THE-HEDGE ground ivy.

ROUNDED in teaspoon or tablespoon, as much heaped above the rim of the spoon as below.

ROXBURY RUSSET greenish to yellowish-brown apple; origin in Roxbury, Mass., 1649.

ROYAL CIDER hard cider spiked with applejack.

RUBBERY an undesirable aroma that afflicts wine containing an excess of hydrogen sulfide.

RUMBOOZE ale, wine, sugar, and eggs.

RUMBOWLING rum.

RUMFUSTIAN strong beer, sherry, gin, eggs, and spices.

RUMSWIZZLE a mixture of ale and beer.


SABLES sandy soil.

SACCHARIFY to convert into sugar.

SACK a dry, light-colored wine akin to sherry.

SACK-MEAD mead with brandy and hops.

SACK-POSSETT sack, sugar, milk, eggs, and nutmeg.

SALTSPOON ⅛ of a teaspoon.

SCION a shoot or small branch.

SCOTCHEM a mixture of hot applejack and mustard.

SCRUPLE 20 grains apothecary.

SEVEN-WATER-GROG contemptuous name for a very weak drink.

SHEEPNOSE see *black gilliflower.*

SILLABUB hot spiced hard cider with heavy cream.

SIPHONING see *racking.*

SIR WALTER RALEIGH'S POSSET ale, sherry, and cream.

SLUG OF BLUE FISH HOOKS applejack.

SMOKEHOUSE yellow or red apple; origin in Lancaster County, Penn., early 1800's.

SNOW see *fameuse.*

SOMMELIER a wine waiter.

SOPS OF WINE dark crimson red apple imported very early from England.

SOUND having suffered no putrid fermentation.

SOURING vinegar fermentation.

SPAETLESE wine made from late-picked grapes.

SPARGING rinsing.

SPICY herblike, rich smell often encountered in white dinner wines.

SPILE a wooden spigot; a wooden or small metal tap for taking the sap from trees.

SPIRITS alcohol.

SPLITTING HEADACHE ale, rum, lime juice, and spices.

SPRING SHATTERING the partial destruction of berry-producing flowers by spring frosts, hail, or inclement weather.

STEWED QUAKER hot cider plus applejack with a hot roasted apple floating in it.

STICK stop the fermentation before all the sugar has been converted to alcohol.

STILLAGE a stand for casks.

STILLION a vessel to receive the yeast that is drained from a barrel.

STILLIONS the supports for a barrel.

STINGO strong beer.

STOMACH the odor given off during fermentation.

S T O N E  W A L L hard cider, apple brandy, brown sugar, and spices, served hot. Sometimes made with rum, omitting the brown sugar.

S U D S see *homebrew.*

S U G A R  L O A F or C O N E, 9 to 10 pounds of sugar.

S W E A T I N G air-drying apples.

S W E E P  P R E S S a press for cider using the mechanical advantage of a wooden bar instead of a screw.

S W E E T  B O U G H greenish yellow apple; origin in America, early 1800's.

S W I T C H E L beverage strengthened with rum.

S Y L L A B U B body-heat red or white wine, ale or cider, milk, sugar, and spices.

S Y M P O S I U M a drinking together usually following a banquet, with music, singing, and conversation.

T A B L E S P O O N a dry or liquid measure;

1 tbls. = ½ ounce
= 3 teaspoons.

In old recipes = 4 teaspoons.

T A M M Y sieve. T O  T A M M Y to strain through a tammy.

T A N N I N an essential preservative acquired from the skins, pips, and stems of grapes during the initial fermentation and later from the wood of the casks.

T A R T A R I C  A C I D one of the most important fixed acids in grapes and subsequently in wine. It is rapidly decreased by oxidation either during fermentation or when wine is exposed to air.

T A R T R A T E S crystal deposits made up of potassium bitartrates which precipitate to the bottom of the bottle or which attach themselves to the bottom of the cork. Their presence signifies that the wine has been chilled at least once in the bottle.

T I L L E R side sprout of a corn stalk.

TUN a 250 gallon barrel.

TO TUN to put into a barrel.

TWOPENNY a pale, small beer.

ULLAGE the amount a vessel lacks of being full.

VARIETAL wine named after grape or apple from which it is made.

VINIFICATION the winemaking process from ripe fruit.

VINTAGE the harvesting of the grapes and the wine made from that particular year's picking. Every year is a vintage year and all wines are vintage wines as long as they are made from the juice of grapes or fruit picked in a single year and not blended with grapes or fruit of an earlier year.

VINTNER one who sells wine.

VITICULTURE the science or art of grape-growing and cultivation.

WAGENER bright red apple with contrasting yellow; origin in Penn Yan, N.Y., about 1800.

WALNUT SIZE 2 tablespoons.

WASSAIL hot ale, sherry, apples, toast, and spices. The name comes from the Welsh and Anglo-Saxon "waes hael" = "be well."

WATER SEAL fermentation lock, air lock, water valve.

WATER VALVE see *water seal.*

WELLINGTON BLOOMLESS yellow apple; origin in England, early 1800's.

WEY a dry measure: 1 wey = 40 bushels.

WHISTLE-BELLY-VENGEANCE sour beer, molasses, bread crumbs; drunk piping hot.

WHITE MEAD see *bragot.*

W I L L I A M S a bright red apple overlaying yellow; origin in Roxbury, Mass., about 1760.

W I N D Y flatulent, apt to generate gas in the alimentary canal.

W I N E , D E S S E R T wine with pronounced sweetness.

W I N E , F O R T I F I E D wine in which the alcoholic content has been raised by additives, usually a brandy. About 20 percent alcohol.

W I N E , S O U R caused by partial conversion of wine to vinegar or, technically, alcohol to acetic acid—a process known as acetification.

W I N E , T A B L E a wine of medium alcoholic content and very light sweetness. About 11 percent alcohol.

W I N E C R A D L E a device usually of wire or wicker, arranged so that the bottle is kept on its side with the neck elevated about 15° so that the wine may be poured with a minimum disturbance to the lees.

W I N E G L A S S ¼ cup.

W O O D P E C K E R see *baldwin.*

W O O D Y the characteristic odor of wet wood which is apparent in wines aged for a long period in wooden casks.

W O R T pronounced "wert"; from the German *würze.* The fermenting liquid making beer.

Z Y M U R G Y the branch of applied chemistry that deals with fermentation processes.

# Wines & Beers of Old New England

# CHAPTER ONE

# Why was it important?

The early American farmer must have been thirsty most of the time. His physical work was hard and continuous, his food was heavy and contained a great deal of starch. More than that, his food was preserved by the thirst-provoking methods of drying, smoking, and salting. Small wonder that his liquid intake was reported as prodigious. Although some of the reports can scarcely be believed—the survey of Massachusetts in 1767 estimated cider consumption at more than a keg (about 5 gallons) a day for each person—all signs point to a very thirsty population. What to drink was a major problem. Sixteenth and seventeenth century European farmers had known for generations that milk was very dangerous for adults and children alike. Cows particularly gave people the dread "milk sickness" (tuberculosis), and in New England water soon took on the same sinister characteristics.

Two typically New England facts brought about polluted water: Indians and the weather. Even when the farmer was not fearful of attack from his native neighbors, experience gave the Indians a reputation of such unreliability that the stealing of animals and children was an ever-present worry. When the barn and house were attached, these threats were greatly reduced. Even when Indians were not around, common sense dictated that in winters of deep snow the least shoveling of snow the better. Wells were either next to the house, usually in an attached shed, or right inside. Sanitary requirements were unknown. The customary way of dealing with human wastes was to use a "chamber pot," which was emptied onto the animal dung heap, often very close to the water supply. Yet the farmers needed to quench their thirst, and although secondarily the alcohol in beer, wine, and cider must have helped to make the rugged unpleasantness of their lives more endurable, primarily the alcohol was a preservative for their drinks.

The colonials praised their beverages as aids to health and well-being, and with our present-day knowledge we can see that they were right. Take beer, for example. The nutritional and medicinal values of spent yeast (left over from the brewing process) had been recognized for centuries. Since colonial beers were not clarified but were murky and muddy with yeast, they supplied many of the vitamins and minerals needed for good health.

Although the food value of the beer the farmer drank was an important asset, it is impossible to quantify it, since we have no exact records of how much was consumed. Travelers, diarists, and reformers all wrote of the vast quantities of alcoholic beverages that New Englanders drank, and there are some records of how much was consumed in a particular tavern or town, but how much the farmers made and drank themselves is just not documented. Studies of modern premachinery farming societies show, however, that beer can be an important part of their diet. For example, in the hills of Tibet where the climate is not unlike New England, between one third and one half of the daily caloric input of a hard-working farmer comes from the beer he drinks. Such studies support the idea that beer in particular was important as a food in the Colonies.

Long before any Europeans had pushed inland to settle America, wine was held in high regard as a healthful and almost necessary drink, and for the pious farmer the Bible had many praises for its use. Obviously too much wine was not good for anyone. A rough rule of thumb one often finds in old books is the recommendation of one quart a day per person. A great list of ailments was advertised as being helped by "the nurse of old age." Wine was supposed to strengthen the heart, to alleviate hay fever, gangrene, hardening of the arteries, nervous breakdowns, and insomnia, and to ease childbirth, and hot wine was said to be particularly good for curing bronchitis. Modern studies show that wine could in fact have been supplying the colonials with vitamins and trace elements essential to their well being. With neither the knowledge nor the availability of the food supplements we now feel to be essential, hundreds of generations learned from experience that wines and beers were important to their health.

But where to get these benign beverages in a cold—and, to some, forbidding—land of forests and mountains? The early settlers brought their malted barley and their wine with them, but to rely on supplies from England was clearly too expensive and too uncertain. Almost as soon as they had landed, the newcomers started to explore the forests and to test the land. They soon discovered that their forests abounded in grapes. Vines with trunks as thick as a man's arm disappeared up into the treetops seeking the sunlight at the top of the great forests. Berries of all sorts covered the clearings made either by the Indians or by fires set by lightning. Hops grew wild in the woods, and when the land was tilled, barley grew well in the soil and climate.

The real problem was sugar, which was essential to the wine-making process. New England is far too cold for sugar cane, and sugar beets were not developed until the turn of the nineteenth century. Importing sugar was much more than the farmers could afford, so the story of colonial New England's wines, beers, and ciders is primarily the story of how New England developed the sugars that must be present if fermentation is to take place.

# CHAPTER TWO

# Where did the sugar come from?

The earliest settlers brought everything with them, and even after they began to farm, they relied for their sugar, molasses, and malt on what ships could bring from England. Although the British government required that colonial-bound cargos must touch at an English port before being sold in the colonies, the New England merchants, as time went on, paid less and less attention to this law. The colonial shipping industry grew, and more and more American ships went southward to the West Indies, where sugar was so plentiful that these Indies became known as the Sugar Islands. Even this sugar cost more money than the common farmer could afford, however, and he used very little of it.

There was another reason. By the early eighteenth century a most lucrative trade had been discovered that was making both merchants and seamen wealthy, based primarily on sugar and molasses. The New England merchants imported the sugar, turned it into rum, and sent the rum to Africa to be exchanged for cargoes of slaves. Most of the slaves were taken to the islands in the West Indies for work in the sugar plantations. On their home voyages the ships brought back sugar and molasses for the New England distilleries. This piled up great fortunes for the operators but affected the kitchen larders of the common people very little. More than that, it was an industry fraught at times with violent conflict, which added greatly to the tensions that were to culminate in the Revolution.

But it was not just the tug-of-war between British and American financial and political interests that so jeopardized the imports of sugar. There was a deep and at times overpowering revulsion felt by the ordinary colonial New Englander against the slave trade. Slaves and sugar were so tied together that consumer boycotting of sugar became at times almost a religious as well as patriotic duty.

As is well known, the use of slaves was lawful in New England. The wealthy and the well-to-do commonly had slaves, both negro and Indian, and they were a regular part of family living. It was the slave trade from Africa as a link in the rum and sugar business that so disturbed the consciences of the common people. Time and again religious and political reformers whipped up public indignation that would sometimes result in an almost complete boycott by consumers of sugar and molasses.

It is little wonder that the ordinary farmer and laborer never looked on cane sugar as a staple, and turned elsewhere for a more available, more dependable, and cheaper source to assure his supplies for his daily living.

# Honey

Honey is the oldest sugar known to man. In the Spider Cave near Valencia in Spain, Paleolithic men painted two naked people climbing a crude rope ladder to take honey from a cleft in a cliff surrounded on all sides by angry bees. This rock painting, ten to fifteen thousand years old, was made while man was exclusively a hunter. There was no agriculture and hence no other source of sugar. It seems probable that these early men let diluted honey ferment. All through recorded history magical and religious significance has been attached to honey and the honey bee. How else could the transformation in people be explained which occurred after drinking deeply of this remarkable substance?

Honey and the bee have somehow been connected with death or the spirit of the dead since the beginning of recorded history. In colonial America the "telling of the bees" of a death in the family to assure that they would not fly away was a commonly practiced custom among the simple folk. As late as 1858 Whittier's *"Telling the Bees"* commemorates this practice. Mark Twain had old Jim tell Huckleberry Finn, "If a man owned a beehive, and the man died, the bees must be told about it before sun-up next morning or else the bees would all weaken down and quit work and die."

Thomas Jefferson in his *Notes on Virginia* said that "the honey

bee is not a native of our continent. The Indians concur with us in
the tradition that it was brought from Europe . . . The bees have
generally extended themselves into the country, a little in advance
of the white settlers. The Indians therefore call them the white
man's fly; and consider their approach as indicating the approach
of the settlement of the whites."

Jefferson was not quite correct, since the Spaniards reported
honeybees in Mexico, and deSoto's expedition reported so much
honey in Florida and other areas of the South that the first adventurers to New England came expecting to find and use honey to
supplement their sugar supplies. Failing to locate any, they brought
bees with them on their next voyages. One indication that there
were no indigenous honeybees in New England comes from the
early missionaries who translated the Bible into the northern Indian languages. They used the English words "bee" and "honey"
when these terms occurred, although they sometimes fixed them
up with Indian endings.

Bee culture was common in the British Isles, and the pioneer
settlers were quick to establish hives in their settlements. We

know that by 1640 there was a municipal apiary in Newbury, Massachusetts, where bee colonies were selling for five pounds apiece, equivalent to about fifteen days labor for a skilled craftsman. As time went on, more and more of the hives swarmed, and it was not long before the nearby forests were populated with "wild" colonies. Bees do not thrive in the forest, however. Open fields, where flowers soak up the sunshine, and orchards, where the land has been cleared to give fruit trees room to grow, are where most bees are to be found. Thus as the settlers cleared the forest for their own farming, they provided the magnet for the growing bee population that escaped from the imported hives.

The early farmers did not try to maintain a continuous supply of honey, although they did search out bee colonies settled in hollow trees or rock crevices or caves. They knew that nectar-laden bees flew in straight lines to their hives; and when they had the time, the farmers or, more likely, their children spent many hours watching the flight of bees to locate a hive. The technique was to smear honey on the inside of a small box with a lid, put it out, open, in a field where bees were working and observe the direction of flight of the bees that came to feed from the box. When a dozen or so bees were feeding in the box they would clap down the cover, pick up the box and move it down the bee-line as far as they were sure of, set the box down, open it up, and repeat the process. By this technique, it might take a person two or three days to locate a wild hive, if indeed it could be located at all. However, if they could bring home fifteen or twenty pounds of honey, an average yield, much less work would have been involved than in making an equivalent amount of maple syrup, the other most common form of sugar for family use.

When a honey tree was located, it was chopped down and split open, and the combs removed. The farmer might look for the queen, to transfer her to a straw or wicker basket which would serve as a hive on the edge of his cultivation, but usually the early settlers were eager to get the honey, not the bees. Having chopped down the tree, their usual method was either to plug up the entrance to the hive tightly enough to smother the bees or to maintain a smoky fire at the entrance long enough to drive the bees out.

They also used sulphur smoke, if they had it available, which would poison the bees and kill them in the hive. The reason was that although bees while being tracked are benign, they are vicious as soon as their hives are threatened, and the settlers did not have the sting-proof equipment now universally employed by anyone handling bees.

In gathering honey from their own hives, colonial farmers made little effort to save the bees. Common practices were to suffocate the hive with sulphur smoke, or, the hives being for the most part straw baskets, to cut the hive apart, releasing the honey but in the process drowning a large part of the colony. They also employed the method of "driving," according to which an empty hive-box was put on top of a full one and cloth or leather smoke was blown into the door of the lower one. They thus drove the bees upward into the empty hive. Sometimes the bees stayed in the upper box and sometimes they did not, but the object was to get at the full honeycombs in the lower hive and only secondarily to keep the bee colony.

The honey was removed by cutting the comb into small pieces and hanging it up near a fire or in the sun, enclosed in a rough cloth bag or closely woven basket to let the warm honey drip out. Or the whole chopped-up hive was put in a press and the honey squeezed out. To remove the residue of the honey the comb mass was "washed" by soaking it in water to dissolve what honey was left. This diluted honey would be of such a concentration that it would quickly ferment and it was used to make metheglin, a type of mead well treated with herbs and spices, to cover up odd tastes coming from all of the non-honey components left in the comb.

The wax, an important product of the hive, had to be separated from the debris—wood, straw, dead bees and larvae, and other accumulated junk. To do this, a common method was to tie all the remains in a cloth bag, put in a few pebbles so that the bag would sink, and place the bag in a large pot. Water to cover the bag was added, and the pot hung over a fire. As the heat increased, the wax melted and floated to the top, where it was skimmed off and the refuse in the bag was discarded.

# How to Be a Bee Hunter

There is a group of hardy outdoor sportsmen whose specialty is bee hunting. If you really want to see how it is done you should go along on one of their expeditions. They have specialized bee boxes with sliding panels, partitions, and windows where the light can be adjusted to move the bees around inside the box to control their behavior. They also have sophisticated bee-handling equipment.

But if you just want to experience the early settlers' technology and spend a few days in the open countryside with your family or friends, all you need is a simple box with a tight-fitting cover, which can be slapped down to capture a few bees, and a great deal of patience. Your only real decision will come if you are successful and actually find a honey-tree. When running a bee-line, there is almost no chance of getting stung. The bees are so busy with the nectar you are giving them that unless you go out of your way to annoy them, they will leave you strictly alone. On the other hand if you start sawing down a bee-tree, cracking it open, and stealing the honey, they will turn their full fury on you to repel the invasion.

One factor to be aware of is that there are few areas in New England today where you can run a bee-line without ending up in a farmer's apiary. If you are really after a honey-tree, spend some time mapping out farms and beekeepers. There are only two months in the summer when there is enough vigorous bee activity to make bee hunting worth while: July, when the milkweed is blooming, and September, when the goldenrod is out. Good warm days are also essential. Find an old gray piece of comb—it can be from a wasp's nest as well as from a bee's hive—and fill the cells either with diluted honey or sugar solution (1 cup of sugar to 2 cups of water). Place this bait in a box with a hinged cover. Put the box, open, in a field full of active bees, then go away for an hour or so. There is no point in watching the bees when they first start to find your nectar. Until they have your trap well located, they fly around in circles and figure-eights, getting their bearings. It is not until they have made several trips to the hive that they establish the straight-line flight pattern. After a suitable time, sit quietly by and watch to see the bees taking off in a particular direction.

It is useful at this point to know how far away the nest is. A bee flies at about the rate of a good distance runner—four minutes to the mile or, if you want to recreate colonial times, 288 pulse beats to the mile for a normal person sitting quietly watching a bee trap. A good estimate is that it takes a bee about two minutes to unload his nectar in the hive, so that if you mark an individual bee you can estimate how long your bee-line is. A dab of any bright coloring will do; modern bee hunters seem to prefer a little blue carpenter's chalk mixed with water. With a small camel-hair brush, mark the rear end of a bee that is concentrating on your nectar with its whole head well thrust into a cell in the comb. When it takes off, start timing. If it is gone ten minutes, that is eight minutes of flight or a mile each way, which is a long but not an impossible bee-line to run. Anything less than that is good. If it is gone fifteen minutes, just quit. It means that even if your marked bee may continue to come back, it will not bring many of its hive-mates with it, and running a bee-line with a single bee is impractical. Take up your box and move it about a mile in the general direction your bee went and start again.

Assuming, however, that your bee comes back in a reasonable time, wait until you have ten or a dozen bees on your loaded comb, snap down the lid of the box, and move it two or three hundred yards down the bee-line that you have already estimated. Open up the box to release the bees and repeat the whole process. If your estimate of the line was not good enough, the bees will not find your trap in its new location. If this happens, take the box back to where you were before and try again. As you get closer to the bee-tree you will attract many more bees from the same hive; the process gets easier and surer, and you will have to refill the comb more and more often. If you overshoot the tree, the line will, of course, reverse. Then you are in good shape to start to look for the tree, although you have probably been spending some of your time looking for it before then. Don't be surprised if the process has taken a couple of days already.

A bee-tree can be very hard to spot because the hive entrance is often high in the tree and at the crotch of a limb not easily visible from the ground, but if you know about where it is, be persistent. The most likely trees are maples, beeches, or hemlocks, although any tree is possible.

If, having found the honey-tree, you are going to "take it up," be sure to wear good bee-handling equipment. The up-until-now very friendly bees will be quite literally fighting for their lives, and you must be properly protected. Saw the tree down and go away for half an hour or so to let the bees settle down. Then examine the tree carefully to see just where the nest is. Probe around the entrance with a brace and bit to find out the extent of the hollow. If the bit comes out covered with honey or rotten wood, you were in the hive. If the bit chips are sound wood, you are above or below the hollow. When you know how big the nest is, saw off this section (with liberal smoking of the bees), pound splitting wedges into the sound wood at either end and split the section open, exposing the comb. You have your honey! If you are very lucky, you may have as much as 100 pounds; if you are very unlucky you may reap a single pound or less, but on the average you should expect fifteen to twenty pounds of strained honey for your trouble and excitement.

If you want bee colonies rather than the honey from the bee tree, remember that such a tree is a continuing source of swarms, so keep track of it through the summer months. Beekeeping is such a common hobby these days that this is not the place to go into details about how to raise bees. The best way to start is to find a friend who is a bee-keeper and let him guide you.

A single colony should produce about fifty pounds of excess honey a year, so that one hive should be ample for your beer and wine needs.

When you use your own honey for increasing the sugar content of beer, wine, or cider, you do not have to extract the honey from the comb. Simply cut up the comb into small enough pieces to go through the neck of the carboy or bung-hole of the barrel in which you are fermenting, and leave the wax as sediment when you make your first separation. If you want to use the wax for making candles (and it makes the very best), you have to remove the honey

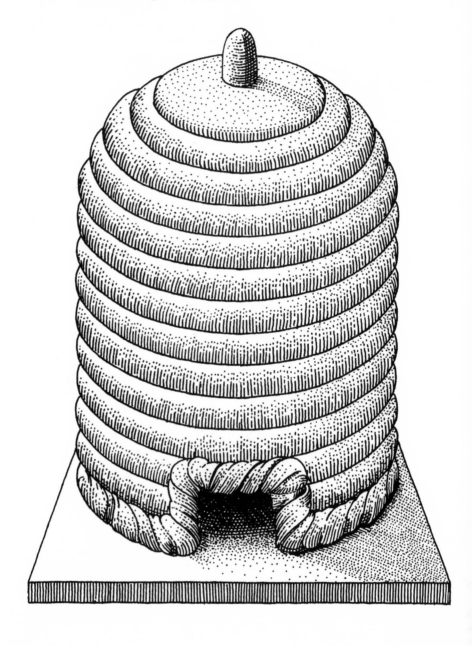

from the comb. What is left as lees after fermentation is an unuseable mess.

Honey was one of the most common sweeteners in colonial New England. It was used in all kinds of combinations and perhaps that is why there is no uniform terminology for beverages made with fermented honey. Even in England, from where the early settlers came, names were not specific even within a single recipe book. For example, in *The Closet of Sir Kenelme Digbie Opened*, published in London in 1669, on page 120 we can find a recipe for "Ale with Honey":

*Sir* Thomas Gower *makes his pleasant and wholesom drink of Ale and Honey thus. Take fourty Gallons of small Ale, and five Gallons of Honey. When the Ale is ready to Tun, and is still warm, take out ten Gallons if it; which, whiles it is hot, mingle with it the five Gallons of Honey, stirring it exceeding well with a clean arm till they be perfectly incorporated. Then cover it, and let it cool and stand still.*

Essentially the same recipe is attributed to Mr. Webb on page 125 under the name of "Bragot":

*To make Bragot, He takes the first running of Ale, and boils a less proportion of Honey in it then when He makes His ordinary Meath . . . As for Example to twenty Gallons of the Strong-worth, he puts eight or ten pounds, (according as your taste liketh more or less honey) of honey.*

Many of the old recipes for beer made with honey called the drink "mead," "malt mead," or "bragot." True mead in the modern terminology is solely fermented honey, what was called in old New England "white mead." Regardless of what it was called, throughout the area any farmer with extra honey who wanted his beer to keep better and who preferred it strong, added what honey he could spare to the wort of his beer and produced an excellent drink. Also, as we will see, native New England grapes do not have enough sugar in the ripe berries to produce a good wine, and honey was a common supplement to the juice to assure a good fermentation into wine.

# Meads

Besides using honey for increasing the sugar content of beers, ciders, and wines, the colonials made wine directly from honey. Although there are plenty of yeasts mixed with raw honey, fermentation cannot take place at sugar concentrations above 30 percent, and since honey is about 80 percent sugar, the virgin honey keeps very well. The bees know this. When they fly into the hive with a load of nectar, they fan it with their wings to evaporate the water until the sugar concentration is high enough to prevent fermentation!

In addition to the meads just described, the early New Englanders made three other kinds. When the honey was just diluted with water, usually rain water, before fermentation, it was called "mead." If the honey was fermented with fruit juices like apple, pear, raspberry, blackberry, currant, or the like, it was called "melomel," and if either mead or melomel were spiced, it was known as "metheglin."

To make simple mead, honey was diluted with one part honey to four parts water (or "add honey to the water until it will bear [float] an egg"), yeast was added if it did not start to ferment by itself, and the liquid was stored in a barrel with a loosely bunged hole until it was still. It was then taken off into bottles or jugs and sealed up. To improve the keeping quality, the water was often boiled with hops, which was removed before the honey was added. This was likely to be called "hop mead." There are many references to flavored meads—"walnut mead" (2 dozen walnut leaves per gallon), "barley mead" (½ pound barley per gallon), "sarsaparilla mead" (¼ pound sarsaparilla per gallon). It is clear that the farm-wife, who was usually in charge of making the meads and beers, felt free to strengthen the tastes of her meads with any local herb that struck her fancy.

In making melomel, honey was added in a one-to-three ratio to any fruit or berry juice that was in abundant supply at the time.

When it comes to metheglin, there were almost as many different spices used as there were families that made it, with each person bragging of his or her particular combination of mace, nutmeg, cinnamon, ginger, pepper, sweetbriar, rosemary, hickory leaves, or other readily available herbs. In Sir Kenelme Digbie's book, which was a very popular cookbook among the wealthier colonials, there are eighty-nine different recipes for metheglin. To illustrate the abandon with which spices were added, here is a quote from one of them:

*Take two handfuls of Dock (alias wild Carrot) a reasonable burthen of Saxifrage, Wild-sage, Blew-button, Scabious, Bettony, Agrimony, Wildmarjoram, of each a reasonable burthen; Wild thyme a Peck, Roots and all. The Garden-herbs are these; Bayleaves, and Rosemary, of each two handfuls; A Sieveful of Avens, and as much Violet-leaves: A handful of Sage; and three handfuls of Sweet-Marjoram. Three Roots of young Borrage, leaves and all; Two handfuls of Parsley-roots; Two Roots of Elecampane: Two handfuls of Fennel: a peck of Thyme; wash and pick all your herbs from filth and grass.*

These were all to be boiled in water until "you may easily slip off the skin of your Field-herbs, and that you may break the roots of your Garden-herbs between your Fingers." These were then strained out, honey added until "it will cause the Egge to ascend upwards, and to be on the top as broad as six-pence" and put into a "tun" (a 250 gallon barrel) to ferment.

Mead, melomel, and metheglin were drunk either hot or cold, and a steaming mugful of metheglin on a cold winter night was believed by the early settlers to be a safeguard against chill and fever.

# Try It Yourself

A recipe published in *The Country Housewife* in 1762 is easy to follow if you want to make mead in an old-fashioned way:

*Take eight Gallons of Water, and as much Honey as will make it bear an Egg; add to this the Rinds of six Lemmons, and boil it well, scumming it carefully as it rises. When 'tis off the Fire, put to it the Juice of the six Lemmons, and pour it into a clean Tub, or earthen Vessel, if you have one large enough, to work three days, then scum it well, and pour off the clear into the Cask, and let it stand open till it has done making a hissing Noise; after which stop it up close, and in three months time it will be fine, and fit for bottling.*

You may not want to play around with the egg trick or you may not be able to if you do not have access to a freshly laid egg. A hydrometer is the modern equivalent; the proper specific gravity should be around 1.100. The result is three pounds of honey per gallon for a dry mead and up to five pounds for a sweet one. On the assumption that your drinking water is safe, you don't have to boil the water unless it is heavily chlorinated, in which case you should do so to remove the chlorine taste.

As has been mentioned, hops was often introduced into mead because it is a good preservative. If you want to try this, use ¾ of an ounce of dried hops per gallon, putting the hops in a cheesecloth bag and boiling it in the water for half an hour. Then remove the bag and add the honey.

If you use your own honey or any honey that has not been sterilized, there will be enough yeast available to start fermentation. This is particularly true if you use honey still in the comb. The early farmers were not fussy about their yeasts. They used the dregs of former fermentations (wines, beers, meads) or, very commonly, bread yeasts. Ordinary dried baker's yeast works fine. An all-purpose wine yeast will also work well.

Under no circumstances follow the above recipe so far as "let it stand open till it has done making a hissing Noise." That would be to ask for trouble, particularly if you are making only a gallon or so. To be sure you get wine instead of vinegar, seal the liquid with a fermentation lock (see below, page 74). The colonials did not know what fermentation really was and so often had failures in their wine making, but though we are trying to reproduce old

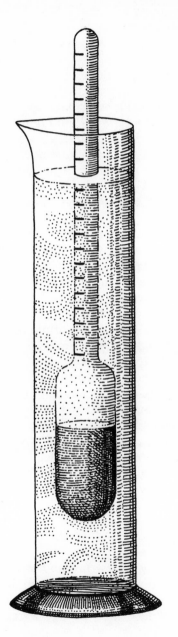

*A Hydrometer*

wines, there is no reason why we should reproduce failures along with successes.

A good recipe for making melomel:

> *1 gallon fresh apple cider*
> *3 pounds dark liquid honey*
> *Spice bag containing:*
> *2 sticks of cinnamon*
> *1 nodule of ginger root*
> *6 whole cloves*
> *1 package of dry yeast.*

Heat the cider to the boiling point and add the honey and the spice bag. Keep the mixture just below the boiling point for twenty minutes. Remove the spice bag and skim the liquid to remove the foam and floating debris. When it cools to lukewarm, add the yeast, pour it into a jug, and seal it with a fermentation lock. At room temperature it will take about three months to ferment. Bottle it when it is still and try to wait a year before drinking. This is a very good drink served hot on a cold winter's night.

Use the same recipe to make metheglin, replacing the cider by water and using your own imagination to choose the spices. Common ones to use were—besides cinnamon, ginger, and cloves—mace, nutmeg, peper, marjoram, and mustard. The farmers also made a much less spicy metheglin from the leaves of various trees. If you want to try this, stay away from any of the strong spices. Use two ounces per gallon of bruised leaves. Hickory leaves will produce a nutty taste, black birch leaves (or bark) will result in wintergreen, and oak leaves will add a touch of bitterness.

# Maple Sap

The sugar most typically a New England product comes from maple trees, the sap of which, as is well known, has a peculiar behavior in the early spring. If the tree is tapped, the sap runs out of holes in the bark, provided that the tree warms up above freezing

*A present-day maple tree*

*Indian method of tapping*

during the day and freezes at night. In New England this means there are about six weeks in the late winter and early spring, at the time the snows are beginning to melt, when a great deal of sugar-bearing sap is available for the labor of collecting it.

The Indians taught the settlers how to tap the maple trees and extract the syrup and sugar. Since it was a great novelty to travelers and diarists who commented on the new and strange American

*Settlers' "boxing" method of tapping*

lands, we have a wealth of old descriptions of how it was done. The earliest method was by means of an axe or tomahawk. A maple tree would be located in the woods, and a man standing on his snowshoes would make a gash in the trunk about six inches long and three inches wide at about the level of his knees. Swinging an axe from a standing position would produce a sloping notch from the lower end of which the sap would drip from a slip or wood stuck into the bottom of the gash. Tapping a tree very many times this way would seriously damage the tree, but this made very little difference to the Indians. The forests were full of maple trees, and if a few died there were lots more.

The settlers, who had metal chisels which the Indians did not have, developed another way of tapping which was considerably more sophisticated and did not damage the trees so much. It was called "boxing". A good description of the technique was sent to the Royal Society of London by Paul Dudley in 1723: "An Account of the Method of Making Sugar from the Juice of the Maple Tree in New England."

*Maple Sugar is made of the Juice of Upland Maple, or Maple Trees that grow upon the Highlands. You box the Tree, as we call it, i.e. make a hole with an Axe, or Chizel, into the side of the Tree, within a foot of the Ground; the Box you make may hold about a Pint, and therefore it must shelve inwards, or toward the bottom of the Tree; you must also bark the Tree above the Box, to steer or direct the juice to the box. You must also Tap the Tree with a small Gimblet below the box, so as to draw the Liquor off. When you have pierced or tapp'd your Tree, or Box, you put a Reed, or Pipe, or a bit of Cedar scored with a Channel, and put a Bowl, Tray, or small Cask at the Foot of the Tree, to receive your Liquor, and so tend the Vessels as they are full.*

It was only a simplifying step to go from boxing to the modern method of tapping by drilling directly into the tree without cutting the box. This was a later innovation and it required a much bigger drill than "a small Gimblet." There is, however, a basic difference between boxing and tapping which depends very much on the farmer's approach to the whole maple sap crop. The early settlers wandered around the forest looking for maple trees, and when they found one, they wanted to maximize the production from a single tree. Boxing produced a lot of sap; furthermore, as the gash dried up, the box could be enlarged to expose new wood, and the tap could be rejuvenated. The Indians, as well as those who boxed their trees, started their sap collecting much earlier than is done today, in the middle of winter if a thaw set in. They collected as much as they could until a thaw was over and then, if the gash or box dried up before the weather turned warm again, they just enlarged the cut to expose new wood to start it running again.

The tomahawk slashing of maple trees was a lot of work but the reopening of old slashes was much easier. So the Indians tended to return to the same trees year after year, enlarging the slash only by removing the healing bark on the top of the slash to get the sap flowing. Eventually, of course, the notch became so big that the tree was weakened and ceased to be useful, but this took many years. The settlers did the same thing. Although they modified the chopping technique with their box method, they did not box many trees, and enlarged the box upward year after year until the tree was eventually killed. It was not until farmers started to tap their trees with an auger that they ceased to damage the tree and could get the sap from ornamental as well as forest trees.

Nowadays, the sap is always piped out of a tree through a metal or plastic "spile" or spout. The early farmers, however, whittled spiles out of hardwood, or from the wood of elderberry or sumac bushes. These bushes have good strong woody structures but with pithy hearts that can be easily pushed out to make a wooden tube.

Drilling to insert spiles is a mass production technique. Instead of working hard on a single tree, the farmers planted many trees together, often along roads where they could get to the trees easily. They put in taps late enough in the winter so that the sap did not stop running until the season was over, and they adjusted their yield by the number of trees they tapped.

To get sweet sap one does not have to tap only sugar (also called "rock" or "hard") maples, although this type of tree is the only one used commercially today, because it has the highest sugar content. Other maples have slightly different tastes; but unless you are an expert, you may not be able to tell the difference. One of the very common maples in New England is the red (also called "swamp" or "soft") maple. This type gives very good sap in abundant quantities, and as far as we can tell was used about as commonly by the Indians and early settlers as the sugar maples. It was not until the farmers started to plant their own trees that the sugar maples became dominant. Red maples tend to be "coppice trees," growing in clusters of six to eight trees sharing common roots. This was a great convenience since each trunk behaves like a single tree and could be tapped accordingly, and they all stood together. It is interesting to note that coppice growth is often found in second growth following a fire. As is common in many primitive cultures, the Indians cleared the woods by setting forest fires. By so doing they stimulated clumps of red maple trees convenient for slashing. The second growth following a forest fire in New England favors coppice growth of two other trees of use to the Indians because of their nuts: hickory and oak.

## Try Tapping

The first thing is to find your maple trees. In the winter this is not so easy for a novice, who will have only the bark to go by. On young maple trees the bark is smooth and on old trees it is deeply furrowed. In between it is changing from one to the other. If you are not expert, you can find yourself drilling into various kinds of hickory or ash trees. The best way is to mark your trees when the leaves are turning color in the fall. Then the maple leaves are so distinctive that it is difficult to make a mistake.

The principal difference between the sugar maple leaf and that of the red maple is the shape between the lobes. On the sugar maple the leaves are rounded between the lobes and the leaf does not have sharp teeth, whereas for the red maple there is a sharp angle between the lobes, and it has sharp irregular teeth.

If you don't tap too early in the spring, you can identify the red maple by the characteristic clusters of rounded reddish buds that appear first at the very top of the trees. You may need to use a pair of binoculars to see them, but when you do, you are sure to be looking at a maple, though not a sugar maple (which has slender tapering buds in common with many other trees). The only other New England tree that has buds like the red maple is the silver (sometimes called white) maple, but the silver is easy to distinguish by its long drooping branches. Even if you tap a silver maple

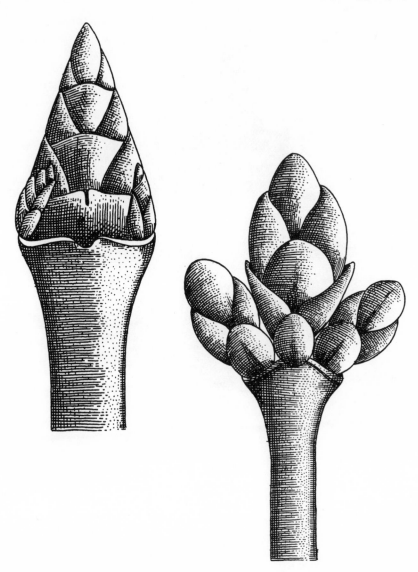

*(L) Sugar Maple Bud, (R) Red Maple bud*

*Sugar Maple Leaf*

*Red Maple Leaf*

by mistake, you will not be disappointed in its sap, although it does not run very well. If you are doing your tree selection when the leaves are on the trees, you will see that the silver maple has leaves that are deeply cut between the lobes and are silvery underneath.

Before you tap, you must have spiles. Metal spiles are readily available in country hardware stores, along with the proper drill sizes to fit the spiles you buy. Any maple tree eight inches in diameter or over can be successfully tapped. The spiles should be set on the sunny side of the trees and the number of spiles you can put in a single tree depends on its size. A rough rule of thumb that has been passed down for generations is that a healthy number of spiles in a tree is its diameter in inches divided by eight.

Drill the tap holes about three inches into the tree. The holes should slope slightly downward, three or four feet above the ground (not the snow) level. Drive the spile in hard with a mallet or hammer. You can hang buckets either on the hooks supplied with the spiles or connect them with plastic tubes to jugs or buckets resting on the snow or ground. Don't use glass, for if the sap freezes, glass jugs will break. The simplest thing is to use open pails. If it happens to rain or snow, either pull in the pails until it stops or just boil the sap a little longer.

To recreate a more colonial atmosphere, you should make your own spiles. This can easily be done from the wood of a staghorn sumac bush. Choose a branch of the right diameter to fit the drill size you are going to use. Whittle off the bark and push out the pith with a stiff wire. The wood is strong, and with a little care such a spile will last for years.

Some people are frightened of sumac. The staghorn sumac is the common one in New England, although there is a poisonous variety that goes by various names, such as poison sumac, poison dogwood, or poison elder. You can't make a mistake between the staghorn and the poisonous sumac during sugaring season, for the staghorn has a large fruit cluster consisting of dry, small, red, hairy berries that remain on the tips of the branches all winter. The fruit of the poisonous kind are small whitish or drab berries in a loose cluster that fall off in the late fall. When the leaves are on the

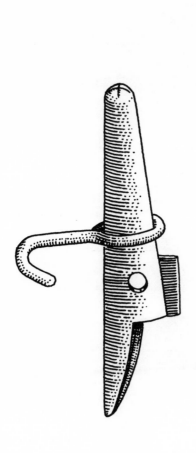

*Spiles*

Staghorn Sumac

bushes, the staghorn sumac has leaves a foot or more long, compound, with ten to thirty sharply toothed leaflets. The poison sumac has seven to ten leaflets without teeth.

If you want to try the Indian method of slashing or the early farmers' boxing method, do it to trees you don't care about. Although the wound will heal on the sides and to some extent on the top of the aperture, the bottom will dry out, crack, and start to rot. Then each year you have to enlarge the slash or box upward to expose new sapwood and downward to reach sound wood to act as a dam for the sap. Eventually this will kill the tree.

# The Running of the Sap

Although the Indians, and their pupils the colonials, were well aware of the requirement of freezing nights and warm days to release the sap, the natural tendency was to correlate the daily weather with the daily yield of sap in the buckets. Such a direct relation seems sometimes to be almost mysteriously absent. Even today a sap farmer will look happily at a warm sunny day following a good freeze and tell you that this is the kind of weather that makes the sap run best. Yet there are many times when the facts are otherwise, and then he will just shrug his shoulders and tell you that the whole process is as unpredictable as the weather.

The hydraulic system of a maple tree is far from understood in all of its details, but enough is known so that we can explain the spring sap flow in a general way. The tree must be able to draw large amounts of water up from its roots, which are below the frost line. It does this by means of a most efficient pumping action resulting from the alternate freezing and thawing of the sap.

Maple tree sap expands very much when it freezes and as it expands, the pressure inside the tree drops to a few pounds per square inch below the atmospheric pressure. Thus when the sap starts to melt, large amounts of water are drawn into the roots and up throughout the tree by this reduced pressure. The roots are semipermeable membranes for the sap. Water can come in, but when it has dissolved the sugars stored in the tree cells, the sap cannot run back out. As the tree warms up, the pressure in the tree increases and can get as high as 20 lbs. per square inch (the atmosphere is around 14 lbs.) at a temperature of 50°F. It is obvious that if you drill a hole in the trunk, the sap will be forced out under the action of this pressure. It takes some time for the sap to move around within the tree, and one good freeze can draw in enough water to keep the sap running for three or four days.

Sap will flow as long as the tree freezes, but as soon as the freezing-thawing pumping no longer occurs, the pressure differential between the sap in the tree and the outside drops essentially to zero. The normal "transpiration" cycle of a tree is maintained by osmotic pressure, which carries on during all of the growing season. This pressure is so slight that the tap holes dry up, and in fact they bark over in a very few years and disappear completely.

Collecting the sap was an arduous and time-consuming process for the colonial farmers. (It still is.) For every gallon of maple syrup, forty to fifty gallons of sap had to be collected and carried to where it was to be boiled. This often had to be done on snowshoes in the deep snow. Large open tubs mounted on a sledge pulled by oxen brought the sap to the boiling place, but these tubs were filled by the farmer, his family, and helpers, who went from tree to tree emptying the individual tree collections into two or three gallon wooden pails hung from a shoulder yoke. Why did they not just carry the pails in their hands and be done with the yokes? The answer is that maple trees seem to grow best on steep New England hillsides, and snowshoeing through this type of terrain with heavy pails of sap requires all the equilibrium possible. A free arm to wave or an available hand to grab a tree or branch to keep one's balance is an essential requirement. Without a yoke one could only carry one pail at a time. The yoke doubled the carrying capacity.

The sap that comes from a maple tree is mostly water, and the sugar has to be concentrated 40 to 1 to make maple syrup. This is done by continued boiling. Metal kettles were one of the greatest boons that the early settlers brought to the New England Indians. Up until the coming of the white men, the Indians had no big pots that could be put over a fire, and they boiled the sap in wooden troughs made of logs hollowed out like a dugout canoe. They heated stones in a fire, dropped the hot stones into the sap, and fished out the cooler ones with stick tongs, hour after hour and day after day. A whole village would be thus employed in syrup and sugar making while the sap was running.

Although the Indians did not make beer, the early settlers soon discovered that they could make strong beer from maple sap much more easily than they could make maple syrup (which they called "Indian molasses"). In conjunction with a usual malt wort for small beer, the sap needs only to be boiled down to one half its volume and used in place of water to give an alcoholic content to the finished product of strong or double beer.

There are a number of reports in the old literature about making maple syrup by freezing the water off, but it seems pretty clear that these are not reports from anyone who had tried it. It is true, of course, that water expands greatly when it freezes, rises to the top of the liquid, and can be taken off and thrown away. It is a process that works well for making applejack (as we shall see). But there is a great difference in the behaviors of maple sap and hard cider. Maple sap freezes into a solid block, breaking any rigid container it is in and trapping the sugar as well as the water in its rigid crystal lattice. Hard cider, on the other hand, freezes to a mush of small flat crystals which will not break glass containers and from which you can drain liquid alcohol even at 30°F. below zero. A true separation can be achieved. Another reason why freezing syrup won't work is that the sap does not begin to run until the really cold weather is over. I suspect that the old reporters were doing some wishful thinking or were taken in by leg-pulling natives. On the other hand, if you tap or box for an early thaw and have good cold weather afterward, you can achieve a concentration of a factor of two by freezing and throwing away the ice and this is just the concentration you need for beer making.

When maple beer was made in the old days, it was an early spring beer and was made right along with the syrup and the sugar. This was because sap does not keep well. It molds easily. Its pectin content is high, and if kept for long, it can turn to a soft jelly which inhibits fermentation. However, fresh sap boiled to one half and used in place of water in the usual process of making beer gave the early settlers an excellent strong beer made totally from the products of their own farm. They also made a wine, which they called "maple mead," by boiling the sap to ⅒th, adding yeast, and fermenting.

## Modern Equivalents

If you have a maple tree, by all means tap it. From a reasonably large tree you can get about eight to ten gallons per spile during a season, so it is easy to get lots of sap.

You can make a good "middle" beer (see below, page 77) by using the sap just as it comes from the tree in place of the water in the basic beer recipe given on page 73. Do this fairly soon after you have collected the sap, for, as noted, it does not keep very well. If you want to make a "strong" beer but do not want to spend the time or the fuel to boil, use the sap augmented by half the sugar in the "strong" beer recipe on page 74. To make colonial strong beer, boil the sap to one half its volume and use it in place of both the water and the sugar in the basic recipe for beer on page 73. It makes a good light beer.

To make maple beer at any time of the year except the early spring, boil the sap down to syrup or sugar so that the sugar content will be high enough for it to keep. Syrup results from boiling down the sap to ¼₀th of its volume or until the temperature of the boiling liquid has risen 7°F—that is, at sea level, to 219°F. This is the jelly-makers "sheeting stage." Over a constant heat the syrup starts to rise up and boil over, so watch it carefully. Five taps running for the season will yield about one gallon of syrup. Although you certainly can do this boiling on your kitchen stove, it is an expensive proposition. Present-day farmers who do not go in for making syrup commercially but just for their own family use boil it down in batches in the back yard. If they are running ten spiles to make a few gallons of syrup, this will take on the order of a cord of wood and about three twelve-hour days of boiling. Back yard equipment for doing this is sketched in the figure. It is made from an old oil drum fitted with a pan holding around 10 gallons of sap.

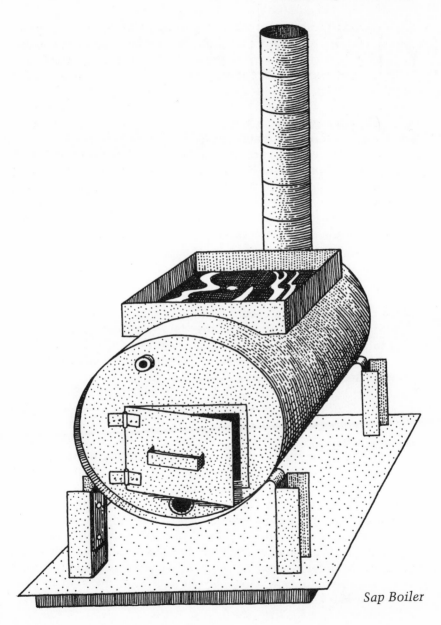

*Sap Boiler*

With a wood fire that cannot be controlled very well, the boiling should not be completed over this outside boiler, but the syrup removed to the kitchen stove to bring it to its final temperature.

Since maple syrup is about one third water, to use maple syrup as sugar for beers, wines, or ciders increase the volume of the syrup by that amount (1½ CUPS SYRUP = 1 cup of cane sugar). If you do not make your own maple syrup, you can still enjoy its great taste, since you can buy pure maple syrup all over New England. Be *sure* that it is 100 percent pure. Artificial syrup will not give a true reproduction. You can, of course, boil all the way to sugar (234°F.) but the final moments of transition from syrup to sugar can go so quickly that it is hard to achieve it without scorching the sugar. It is a lot simpler to stop at the syrup stage, and it is just as good as far as wines and beers are concerned.

# Birch Sap

When the maple trees ceased their flow of sap as the weather failed to dip below freezing in the spring, New England farmers could turn to another tree to provide sugar for making strong beer. This was the birch, which runs its sap for about a month after the temperature stays above freezing. There are several kinds of birches, but by far the best for sugar content is the black birch. This tree—also called, for obvious reasons, the sweet birch—is also known as cherry birch because its dark brown bark makes it almost indistinguishable from the wild cherry. At tapping season it can be clearly recognized by last year's inch-long catkins pointing upward at the end of the branches near the top of trees that are big enough to be useful. It is an interesting fact (and one can wonder whether it was just by chance) that the old rule about not tapping trees smaller than eight inches in diameter corresponds closely to the appearance of these catkins on the tops of mature black trees. They do not occur at all on smaller trees. At any time of the year the black birch can be differentiated from the wild cherry by chewing a twig or a piece of young bark. Hold the chewed bit in the front of your mouth for half a minute or so because it takes a while for the taste

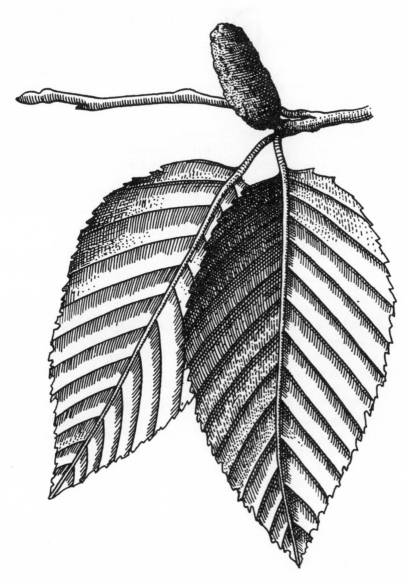

*Black Birch*

to develop. The black birch has a wintergreen taste, and it was from the bark of this tree that early colonials derived their "essence of wintergreen," used as a flavoring.

Since the sap of the black birch runs considerably later than that from the maple, the same spiles used for maple syrup can be transferred to these trees. Birches do not require freezing nights to ensure a copious flow, but the weather needs to be quite warm to get a good run. Birch sap is considerably more dilute, however, and must be boiled twice as long to get the sugar concentration up to maple. At this concentration it has only a faint wintergreen taste, pleasantly subtle in the finished beer.

A much more widespread birch in New England is the white or paper birch. It was also tapped for its sap, though it has a very much lower concentration of sugar and therefore, to be useful, requires a lot more boiling.

# Malt-Birch Beer

Black birches are not as common as maples, but if you can find one, you should try to use it. The flow from a single tree can be copious. Boil the sap to one quarter its original volume and use it in place of both the sugar and the water in the basic strong beer recipe.

To simulate this beer without using birch sap, add 1 teaspoonful of wintergreen extract to the basic beer recipe before fermenting.

If you want to use white birch sap in place of the sugar and water in the basic strong beer recipe, it will have the right sugar content if boiled to one eighth of its original volume. It imparts no noticeable taste to the beer. Boiling white birch sap to a syrup (the same 219°F. as maple syrup) gives a pleasant mild-tasting molasses with a slightly lemony aftertaste. This requires a volume reduction over the original sap of about 150 to 1.

# Birch Beer

The colonials were enthusiastic about birch "beer," which would not be classed as a beer at all in modern terminology, since it was not a malt drink. It was made from black birch sap, birch twigs, and honey. To collect four gallons of birch sap was easy, but it was an amazing amount of work to collect the requisite four quarts of twig buds to provide the flavor for that much beer. It was necessary to take all of the early spring leaf buds from a black birch tree 35 to 40 feet high or about 4 inches in diameter at the butt. Obviously the tree had to be cut down first. If you have the time or this much available labor by friends or family, gather the twigs, put them in the bottom of a large crock, boil four gallons of sap for ten minutes, add a gallon of honey to the sap, and pour the boiling liquid on the twigs. After it has cooled, strain out the buds, add yeast, and ferment.

To get a carbonated beer, do not ferment to completion, but bottle it while it still has a little life. It is slower in fermenting than the standard beers, however, so let it go further toward completion before corking or you may have some broken bottles.

The resulting beer is light and somewhat sweet.

# An Easier Equivalent

Few readers will have either the time or the opportunity to make real birch beer, but there is a completely equivalent way to make it quite easily: Take 5 gallons of maple sap, add to it 2½ quarts (5 pounds) of honey and 2 ounces of wintergreen extract. Ferment in the usual way. The result is an excellent refreshing drink that has an alcoholic strength of about 6 percent.

# Corn

Corn was not a plant native to New England. It seems to have been brought in by the Indians from the Southwest around A.D. 1000.

Roger Williams recorded in 1643 that the Indians had a tradition that "the crow brought them at first an Indian Grain of Corn in one Eare, and an Indian Beane in another, from the great God *Kautantouwits'* field in the Southwest, from whence they hold came all their corne and beanes."

Archaeological evidence indicates that what is now called "eight-rowed northern flint" corn first showed up in New England around A.D. 1400 and was well established in the sixteenth century when Jacques Cartier described extensive corn fields along the Saint Lawrence River in 1535. This type of corn is cold-resistant and can be planted early, "when the white oak leaves are the size of a mouse's ear." It is a bushy plant with many tillers. It is adaptable to cold climates because the concentration of leaves from the tillers at the base of the plant reduces loss of heat from the ground by radiational cooling. The plant also has a reddish coloration, which seems to assist the absorption of radiant energy; that in turn results in leaf temperatures higher than the surrounding temperatures and thus aids greatly in maturing the corn.

The early settlers learned the art of corn cultivation from the Indians, and by archaeological reconstruction combined with contemporary accounts we now have a detailed understanding of how it was done. The Indian technology was remarkably clever. Corn was planted in hills of small stones that were permanently established and used year after year with annual additions of soil and stones. The hills were about a foot high and two feet across and about four feet apart, with two or three plants to a hill. Remains of these Indian corn fields are still to be found in a few places in New England. Travelers in the New England colonies often remarked on the clean cultured condition of the Indian fields which the women and children kept free of weeds by scraping away the top soil between the hills with a shell, bone, or wooden hoe.

The use of stone corn hills is surprising, and several hypotheses have been advanced as to why it was so common among the northern Indians. It may have been for protection of the seed kernels against rodents or birds, or it may have been purposefully used as a rock mulch against weeds, and it certainly does retain the heat during cool nights to speed germination as well as to protect against damage from spring frosts. The wide placement of the hills provided space for the tillers to expand during June and July, nourishing a healthy root system so that early flowering could produce high yields in spite of the short warm season.

One of the most persistent myths of Indian corn culture was that of burying fish in the corn hills to achieve an abundant harvest. According to the records that the Pilgrims have left us, in March of 1621 an Indian strode boldly out of the forest, greeted the settlers with "Welcome Englishman," introduced himself as Squanto and "directed them how to set corn, where to take fish, and to procure other commodities." A letter written the following winter from Plymouth says: "we set spring some twenty acres of Indian corn . . . according to the manner of the Indians, we manured our ground with herring." Ever since then, particularly associated with the "first Thanksgiving" story, our children are reminded of how the Indians achieved an abundant harvest by burying a fish in every corn hill.

Since it is hard to believe that a stone-age native from a hunting culture, on first contact with the Pilgrims, not only could undertake to instruct them in sophisticated farming methods, but also emerge from the forest speaking English, considerable research has been done on this myth to establish the facts. Actually Squanto was a Patuxet Indian who had been kidnapped by Captain Hunt in 1614 and sold into slavery in Spain. From there he was smuggled to London and lived for two years with John Slany, the treasurer of the Newfoundland Company. He was taken to one of the Newfoundland settlements to work as a field hand and to act as a pilot and guide. Eventually he got back to Cape Cod, to find that his tribe had been wiped out by the plague. While he was working in Newfoundland, the Company had been overwhelmed by the abundance of fish to a point where they used them as fertilizer, so Squanto had learned the use of fish from colonists in Newfoundland and was merely passing on his new-found knowledge to the Pilgrims. Nevertheless, independent of the origin and technique, fish were widely used as fertilizer throughout early New England.

Even before the Indians taught the settlers to grow corn, the natives had saved the lives of many British explorers who were probing the coastal wilderness, although God seemed to be given more credit than the Indians. In 1607 Captain John Smith, sailing down the coast and near starvation, wrote: "It pleased God . . . to move the Indians to bring us corn" and thereby keep his party alive. The Governor of the Plymouth Colony, William Bradford, wrote in 1621 that in their desperate winter ordeal they came across corn stored by the Indians "and sure it was God's good providence that we found this corne, for else we know not how we should have done."

The early settlers tried in many ways to adapt corn to their way of life, and they found almost immediately that several parts of the plant could be used as a source of sugar. Just as they learned how to get sugar from the forest trees, the colonials learned from the Indians how to grow corn. The village Indians never invented the plow, and their permanent stone corn hills were incorporated into the village complex. Although the English farmers came with all their experience focused on plowing (and in general they brought their equipment with them), the work of clearing forest land and plowing through tree stumps and the rocky New England soil was terribly hard. It took years to get a field in even reasonable shape. In the meantime, many farmers used the Indian rock-pile method for growing corn for food and drink.

The sugar content of cornstalks is much higher in stalks that for one reason or another do not grow ears. The farmers therefore used only the sterile stalks, or stripped the embryonic ears from the stalks to be used for sugar, before the kernels started to concentrate the plant's sugar.

Landon Carter published one description of the method of extracting the syrup from cornstalks in the *Virginia Gazette* (February 14, 1775):

*The stalks, green as they were, as soon as pulled up, were carried to a convenient trough, then chopped and pounded so much, that, by boiling, all the juice could be extracted out of them: which juice every planter almost knows is of as saccharine a quality almost as any thing can be, and that any thing of a luxuriant corn stalk is very full of it . . . After this pounding, the stalks and all*

*were put into a large copper, there lowered down in its sweetness
with water, to an equality with common observations in malt
wort, and then boiled, till the liquor in the glass is seen to break,
as the brewers term it; after that it is strained, and boiled again
with hops.*

The sugar content of the syrup from the boiled-up cornstalks is
just about the concentration of maple sap, so that to make a strong
beer the syrup was boiled to one half its volume before being used
as the liquid in a malt wort. The corn syrup does not have a strong
taste, so that the beer made with sugar extracted from the stalks is
essentially the same as that made from cane sugar.

# Try It

To get any reasonable yield of sugar in the cornstalks you have to
prevent the ears from maturing. This can be done by pulling off the
infant ears (be careful not to damage the stalks), or by pulling off
the tassels when they are big enough to get hold of but while they
are still pale green, or by covering the ears with paper or plastic
bags so that they will not become fertilized by the pollen.

If you want a genuine reproduction, you should plant eight-row
northern flint seed corn, which is still available occasionally. It is a
"field" corn, not a "sweet" corn, and is not particularly good to eat
as a vegetable, so you lose nothing by preventing all the ears from
maturing to maximize the sugar content of the stalks. If you are
gardening in anything like typical New England soil, you will have
a constant supply of rocks the size of your fist and smaller. Rather
than consider them a nuisance, hoard them as a solar heat storage
reservoir. Pile them, as the Indians taught the early settlers, with
alternate layers of rock and earth and use them as corn hills. If you
use the more conventional earth hills, be guided by the old
farmer's jingle for five kernels to a hill:

> *One for the blackbird,
> one for the crow,*

*one for the cutworm*
*and two to let grow.*

To make a gallon of syrup take three pounds of cornstalks (about six or seven six-foot stalks), cut them into two-inch lengths and break up the fibers by pounding them with a wooden mallet. Boil the pounded pulp for an hour in a gallon of water. Strain and then reduce the volume to one half by further boiling. Use this in place of the sugar and water in the basic beer recipe.

You can make corn sugar beer without growing your own corn stalks, since corn syrup is a readily available commercial product. Since corn syrup is less concentrated than sugar, use 1½ cups of syrup to one cup of cane sugar in the basic beer recipe. It makes a very good beer.

# CHAPTER THREE

# Beer

Beer is a word that is used both generically for all drinks made from fermented grain, and specifically for the malted, brewed, and hopped barley product we are accustomed to today. In fact the early settlers added to the confusion by calling many mildly alcoholic drinks beers even when they contained no grain at all, such as birch beer, root beer, or spruce beer. Historically man has fermented grains as far back as our history and archaeology can probe, but styles in beers have changed rapidly through the years, and it is quite likely that we might find distasteful the beers of even a hundred years ago.

Europe in the seventeenth and eighteenth centuries depended on beers and wines for their liquid intake, since the almost universally polluted water supplies were unfit to drink. The further north one went, the less wine and the more beer was consumed. England was considered an almost exclusively beer-drinking country except for the wealthy aristocracy, which could afford to import wines from the south. Since the early settlers came from England, they came as a beer-drinking people, and in fact beer played a major role in the decision of the master of the *Mayflower* in December 1620 to go no further than Cape Cod. A diary of one of those adventurers (Mourt, London 1622) records that they stopped there because they were already behind schedule and "we could not now take time for further search or consideration, our victuals being much spent, especially Beere." We know further that our pilgrim forefathers started their life in New England without their beer, and complained mightily about it. Governor Bradford, in *Of Plymouth Plantation*, tells us that they "were hasted ashore and made to drink water that the seamen might have more beer."

Perhaps it was because the *Mayflower* was running low on beer that one of the most notable of the pilgrim colony stayed ashore at all. John Alden, by trade a cooper, who had been hired in the ship's company to look after the beer barrels during the voyage and was not intending to be one of the original immigrants, decided at the very last moment to stay with the colonists.

There were, and are, a great variety of "beers"—ales, beers, porters, stouts, etc. The differences were governed by their process of manufacture, and as one would expect, the definition of the terms changed from age to age and from place to place. However, there was an underlying difference between them, and if we restrict our discussion to early New England, we can define the terms fairly specifically once we outline the process of beer making.

The most common source of sugar grown in cold climates for beer was malt. Although most cereals can be malted, the only one that has proven really successful through the ages has been barley. When grain germinates, enzymes are produced that turn the starch into sugar. The process of malting involves letting the grain start to germinate and then heating and drying to stop the process before the sprouts use up the enzymes as the plant grows. Depending on the temperature of the drying, the malt will come out darker or lighter. Dark malts were used in making "stout" and "porter," lighter malts in making "brown ale," "amber ale," "pale ale," "dark beer," and "light beer."

The process of making the malt required a great deal of skill and experience, and even the farmers who made beers from their own barley usually took their grain to a "maltster." Undoubtedly the most famous New England maltster was Samuel Adams, who inherited the family malting business from his father. Although Adams, Jr., forsook the business for politics ten years or so before the Revolution, a "Malt-house" had been in his family since the 1690's.

In any process as tricky as malting, particularly before the days of any scientific understanding of the process, without even a thermometer or temperature control, the final product was extremely variable, and even the commercial brewers had little control of their final product. Early in the eighteenth century the brewers developed the technique of mixing dark and pale malt to achieve uniformity rather than rely on what came directly from the maltster. The acceptance of this mixing led to the first beer technically suitable for mass production, which was called "porter."

The second process in beer making is brewing. The ground malt is boiled and steeped with water (a process called "mashing"); the resulting "wort" is strained and cooled and, with the addition of yeast, fermented. After mashing and straining, the spent grains were an important by-product as cattle feed.

If the result of brewing malt alone was fermented, the product was ale. The original English ale was a sweetish malt wine with an alcoholic content of 10 to 20 percent. It was the Dutch who introduced the hopped malt beverage "beer" into England in the fifteenth century, and gradually the alcoholic content of ale was decreased until the only difference between the two drinks was that beer was hopped and ale was not. The ale was fragile, however, and did not keep well. It was found that brewing the malt with hops greatly improved its storage qualities, so this was almost universally done if the barrels were to be shipped or stored for any length of time. Hopped malt produced beer.

Hops grow wild in New England, but they could not be found everywhere, and the settlers spent a great deal of time and energy trying to find a substitute that would have the same preserving quality. They discovered that spruce was useful in this way and was also tasty, hence spruce beer became very popular in the seventeenth and eighteenth centuries.

Another lack of uniformity had to do with the alcoholic strength of the beer. This was controlled by the length of time the malt was allowed to steep in hot water, and whether the brewer went to the extra expense of adding sugar. The weakest beer, and that commonly drunk in large quantities, was called "small" beer. It used only the sugar from the malt and could be produced very quickly, since its fermentation time was short. It was not aged particularly, and it did not keep very well. It was also sometimes called "single" beer. The best, the most expensive, and the kind that was shipped to and kept in gentleman's cellars was "strong" beer or "double" beer. This was the most alcoholic, the product of brewing the malt for the longest time, and sugar was added to the wort to increase the potency of the result. In between these two extremes were various "middling" beers that went by such names as "table" beer and "ships" beer.

It is not unusual to see old pictures with beer barrels in the background marked with an "XXX". That was a common way of marking beer barrels, not for quality (as some modern myths would have us believe) but for the strength of their contents: "X" was for small beer, "XX" for a middle beer, and "XXX" for strong beer.

The visual appearance of beers and ales has changed markedly since colonial days. Until the middle of the nineteenth century, New England made "English" beers with a yeast that floated on the top of the fermenting wort. These beers were always cloudy, and one of the reasons why hard ciders were considered more elite as a drink was that ciders were clear like wines. With the introduction of "German" beers in the nineteenth century, the public got used to the clear "lager" beers resulting from the fact that German yeasts sink and work from the bottom of the wort. Even though these beers may be cloudy initially, the lees settle out, and even the home beer maker could make what came to be the only socially acceptable appearance—clear beer.

There is quite a bit of evidence to suggest that the shift from English to German beer was stimulated to a large degree by the introduction of clear glass tumblers and mugs. In the early days pewter, pottery, or leather mugs were used. In the middle of the nineteenth century glass became available to the common man, and cider certainly looked more appetizing than the cloudy English type of beer. The manufacturers of German lager beers introduced clarifying and filtering to rival the clarity of cider. Cider making had been a major industry in New England, but because it involved more work and was thus more expensive than lager beer, cider was run completely off the market.

Our modern concept of beer is of a carbonated, foamy liquid which as we have said, is also clear. Neither the carbonation nor the "head" was a requisite of colonial beers. The carbonation was a by-product of the brewers' attempt to guarantee that the beer would not go bad before it was used, for it had been known for hundreds of years that if the beer was kept from the air, it would last indefinitely. Keeping a slight pressure of the $CO_2$ product of the fermentation was the way for assuring no air in the ullage (the empty space at the top of the barrel), but the beer as it was drunk was "still." It was dispensed from nonpressurized barrels in the taverns, and at home it was kept in bottles where the corks would be blown off if any particular pressure were built up over the beer. As for the foam, it had also been discovered centuries earlier that the yeasts need nutrients besides sugar to keep the yeasts actively working, and these often served as contaminants, which resulted in a foaming beer.

# Malt

The process of malting seems to have been developed by the early Egyptians and has been used by people all through recorded history. Malt is sprouted grain, and the most primitive technique of producing it was to plant wheat, barley, or corn in a shallow seed bed, hoe it up when the sprouts had emerged, separate the grain from the dirt, usually in a dried condition, and then wash the malt before grinding. This is the method used by the early Pilgrim in Massachusetts.

A more sophisticated way was to carry out the process not in the ground but where the temperature could be controlled to some extent. Dried barley was steeped in water for two or three days in tanks made of wood, and then the grain was laid out on a "malting floor," often a packed dirt floor in the house cellar. The grain would begin to germinate and was raked over often to keep the germination uniform. In the germination process a necessary enzyme, diastase, is produced. In the growing process this enzyme is used up, so that the aim of malting is to terminate the sprouting process when the enzyme reaches its maximum amount. The old-fashioned maltster's instructions were to take the malt from the malting floor when the tip of the seedlings just reached the end of the husks. The grain was then dried in an oven or kiln to stop further growth. The hotter the roasting temperature, the darker the malt, although care had to be taken not to get the oven too hot or the malt would be "burned" (the enzyme would be destroyed). Around the temperature of boiling water was about right.

From an historical point of view, it is interesting that thermometers were not used for this purpose, even commercially, up until the late eighteenth century, and by the home brewer they were never used. This was not because thermometers were unknown. Meteorological thermometers were used throughout New England since the very early days, but thermometers were not considered necessary in any home-cooking operation.

The new and easy-to-grow grain which the settlers found in their adopted land was Indian corn and many people tried to find a successful method to control its malting. But corn sprouts were much more delicate than those from barley and had to grow much longer before the growth should be stopped. No one was really successful in malting corn. The problem was well described by John Winthrop when he wrote to the Royal Society of London in 1662:

*It is found by experience, that this Corne before it be fully changed into the nature of Mault, must sprout out both wayes a great length the length of a Finger at least, but if more its better, so as it must put out the Roote as well as the upper sprout, and that it may so do, it is necessary that it be laide upon an heape a convenient time till it doth so sprout, but if it lieth of a sufficient thickness for this purpose, it will quickly heate and moulde, if it be stirred and opened to prevent the too much heating of it, those Sprouts that are begun to shoote out (if spread thin) cease growing and consequently the Corne ceaseth to be promoted to that mellowness of Mault. If left thick till they grow any length they are so intangled one in the other and so very tender that the least stirring and opening of the heape breaketh those axells of, and every Graine that hath the sprout, so broken ceaseth to grow to any further degree toward the nature of Mault, and soone groweth mouldy if not often stirred and spread thinn.*

Although the settlers were never able to malt corn successfully, they did use quite a lot of corn in their beer making, as we shall see shortly.

The malt taste has always been an important attribute of beer, and comes from a well-roasted grain. But without the use of a thermometer even the seventeenth and eighteenth century professional maltster produced a product of great variability. This led to many different kinds of beer, and the farmer seldom knew what a particular batch would be like before he tapped a new barrel. The darkest malts gave stout and porter. Lighter malts and mixtures of dark and light brewed brown ale, amber ale, pale ale, dark and light beers. One of the best documented of the dark beers was porter (primarily, I think, because George Washington was partial to it and his many biographers have followed up all kinds of details and minutia). This was made of a mixture of malts in different proportion depending upon the brand. It was dark and bitter but was considered hearty and nutritious and was popular in England and among wealthy gentlemen in America. Until the Revolution it was all imported. After America's independence, porter was one of the main commercial beers made in this country until the introduction of the German lagers. It should be mentioned that as far as the strong beers are concerned, the darkness of the beers was not solely dependent on the malts. Highly refined sugar gave a much lighter beer than the brown sugars, and molasses (which was very comonly used to make strong beer) produced a very dark product.

# The Home Maltster

Just as colonial farmers usually took their barley to be malted by a maltster, so a modern student of old beers will find it easiest to buy his barley already malted. But if you want to try it yourself, here is what you do:

Anyone who has sprouted mung beans, soy beans, or alfalfa seeds already knows how to make malt from barley. Archaeologists may argue that the Chinese started sprouting beans before the ancient Mediterranean peoples sprouted their barley or the other way around, but in any case the origins of malting barley are lost in antiquity. The sugar produced in the brewing process is the oldest of the cultivated sugars, and sprouting to get the enzymes to release the sugar is simplicity itself.

Use unhulled seed barley grain. It takes 2 pounds of malt to make 5 gallons of beer. This amounts to 2 quarts or 8 cups of dry grain, which will swell by a factor of two in the sprouting process, so either do your sprouting in a large ceramic crock or in about one-cup batches, which is easier. Do not sprout in metal containers, but in plastic, china, or glass casserole-type dishes with covers. Be careful to avoid low-fired earthenware, often that coming from Mexico, whose glaze contains poisonous lead sulfate. The best is unglazed pottery, because it holds the moisture necessary for the seeds to mature. An unglazed flower pot with its hole plugged and with some kind of a top works well.

Soak the grain overnight, then drain well. Although sprouts require constant moisture, they will rot if they sit in water. Keep the grain moist, either by using a water-saturated unglazed pottery container or by keeping the sprouts in contact with a moist paper towel. The best sprouting temperature is between 75°F and 85°F. Air must be allowed to circulate around the sprouts, so always leave about one third of the container empty for this, even after the grain has swelled. During the sprouting process carbon dioxide and other gases are evolved. These gases and residues created in the germination process will accumulate and need to be washed away to keep the grain from spoiling, so the barley should be rinsed with warm water twice a day. Be careful to drain it well after each rinsing. The process is completed when the length of the sprouts equals that of the grain kernel. This will take from three to five days depending on the temperature. If the sprouting goes on too long, the enzyme concentration needed for the mashing process to be undertaken next will start to decrease, so watch the sprouting carefully to assure the best results.

To stop the growing process, remove the malt from the sprouting pot and lay the grain out on cookie sheets in the oven to dry. The temperature range for the drying process should be 185°F for a light malt to 230°F for a very dark one. Heating the malt to too high a temperature runs the risk of destroying the enzymes that are necessary in the next process to turn the starch into sugar. Since the yield of sugar is more certain for light malts than for dark, the home maltster should err on the cool side to be sure not to "burn" the malt.

## "Spit" Malt

The enzyme that is produced during the sprouting process—diastase—is readily available in human saliva. Many farm children know the trick of making "chewing gum" from the grains of wheat, rye, barley, or cracked corn by chewing these grains until they stick together in a manageable unit and become pleasantly sweet in the process. This is the same chemistry as ordinary malting.

We can find no records to show that the early settlers knew of this salivary malting process from their own culture. But we know that Indians chewed many different kinds of nuts, roots, fruits, and grains in the preparation of various beverages, and there are some South American Indians who still make a corn beer using salivated grain. We have also heard many stories of "spit" beer, so it is fairly certain that some farmers and their families found it easier to malt by mastication than by sprouting. How widespread the technique was is unknown, but if only corn were available, it would have been the only practical way of malting.

In villages in the Bolivian mountains where this technique is so widely practiced that the beer is made on a commercial scale, large groups of women and children sit around chewing for hours, and a reasonable amount of this malting grain is thus produced. However if a single person does it alone, it is a long and tedious though not unpleasant way of malting. It has the mechanical though not the taste characteristics of chewing tobacco.

## Try It

It takes a little practice to make a salivated malt, but it is interesting to try. Corn was the most common grain used, although wheat, rye, and barley work just as well. Grind the grain into a coarse flour, moisten it slightly so that it can be rolled into a ball about one half to three quarters of an inch in diameter, and pop it into your mouth. Thoroughly work the grain with your tongue until it is well mixed with saliva. The teeth should play very little part in the process. Also, keep your mouth closed, for the warmer you keep the grain, the faster the process. As the malting takes place, the flour coalesces, and it is finished when it will stick to the roof of your mouth so that you can shove it forward with your tongue and remove the mass with your fingers. It takes about 20 minutes. These salivated morsels can be dried and stored until used in the mashing process. They look not unlike plates for false teeth!

As is true in the case of sprouted barley malt, there is more enzyme available in the salivated malt than is used in turning the starch of the malt into available sugar; consequently this malt may be stretched by adding unmalted grain when mashing to make beer.

## Mashing

The enzyme action to change the starch into sugar was made available in the process called "mashing." The malted barley was milled until it was slightly cracked, and this cracked malt, called "grist," was steeped in hot water for several hours somewhat below the boiling point. If the water was too cool, the process did not work, and if it was too hot, acetic acid was rapidly produced which would spoil the beer. The early farmers adjusted the mashing temperature by taste—if too cool, the wort did not become sweet; if too hot, they were warned by the vinegar taste.

Since more enzymes are produced in the germinating process in barley than are required to convert all the starch into sugar, the farmer had a margin of safety in case he did not get the temperature just right. Once he had obtained the enzymes from the malted barley, the surplus could act to turn the starches in unmalted barley, corn, oats, or wheat also into sugar. These untreated grains were often used, since they were cheap and malt was relatively dear. Particularly because corn was so plentiful, cracked corn was often added to the mashing process to conserve the malt. It is clear that the uncertainty in control of the roasting and mashing processes gave a much wider variation in the quality of the beer than any effect of adding unmalted grain to the mash.

## Modern Equivalent

Today the easy way to get malt ready for beer making is not to mash it yourself but to buy it in a can as malt syrup. You can get it this way light or dark, hopped or not hopped. A two and one half or three-pound can is just right to make five gallons of beer. If, on the other hand, you want to recreate the process more authentically, start with malted barley, which you can buy either light or dark. The malt should be cracked with a hand mill set as coarsely as possible. Two pounds of malt cereal will make five gallons of beer. Put it in as much water as can be handled conveniently. (In a modern brewery this is never called "water" but "liquor." In a brewery there is no such thing as water except for washing floors.)

Mashing should be carried out at a temperature of 150°F for six hours. Watch the temperature carefully; for good results it should not vary more than ± 5°. This part of the process smells pretty bad, so be prepared to permeate your house with a fairly heavy odor. After mashing, the spent grain should be rinsed several times in warm water to recover the residue of sugar in the grain—a process that was called "sparging"—and then the whole body of liquor drained from the grain should be boiled to stabilize it by destroying the enzymes and any wild yeasts that are present in the barley malt. The spent grain makes good compost.

If you want to try adding other grains to stretch the malt, use corn, as it was the most common one used in the old days (and in American beers it is still used commercially). Add the dried corn to the malt before milling. A mixture of two thirds malt and one third corn by weight will result in a beer that is almost indistinguishable from an all-malt beer.

# Bread Beer

Making beer from bread has been reported almost since the beginning of recorded history. But to understand what role bread played in the technology of beer making is hard. The whole question is confounded in a maze of inaccurate definitions (what is bread, for example), inaccurate translations (the word for bread and beer often being confused), and inaccurate understanding of the beer-making process. Although somewhat peripheral to our main theme of colonial American beers, a short excursion into the records of beers made from bread even as far back as those written in cuneiform and hieroglyphics gives us some insight into the problem of reconstructing seventeenth and eighteenth century techniques.

The growth of yeasts on starches in air yields carbon dioxide and water, not alcohol. To produce alcohol the yeasts must work on sugar, and in making beers this sugar comes from the enzyme action on the malt in the mashing process. So the question in making bread beers is: where does the sugar come from?

Long before beer was invented, the ancient Babylonians malted barley to increase its nutritional value. The sprouted grain was dried in the sun or in kilns, then ground and formed into loaves or cakes to be eaten as a food. With the discovery of alcoholic fermentation, these loaves or lumps of malted barley were brewed in water, yeast was added, and a beer resulted.

To refer to these loaves or cakes of malt as bread is clearly wrong, although it is done in the literature. Bread by Webster's definition is "a food made of flour or meal with liquid, shortening, and leavening and kneaded, shaped, allowed to rise, and baked." Even if malted barley were used as the flour, the baking process would destroy the sugar-producing enzyme, and alcoholic fermentation could not take place to any extent. However, not only the Assyriologists but also the Egyptologists tell us time and time again that the ancient Egyptians made their beer from barley bread, cut into pieces, soaked in a pot of rainwater, and left to ferment. One can hardly ignore this volume of literature, and in one of the many historical accounts of bread beer James Death (in his *Beer of the Bible*, London, Trubner, 1887) attempts to prove that the leavened bread" of the Bible was really a fermented bread beer.

One of the keys to understanding these records is the "Zosimus Papyrus." Zosimus lived in Egypt around A.D. 300. This papyrus fragment so closely describes the modern Egyptian homemade beer that there is little doubt we can reproduce the recipe. Today's Egyptian peasant takes coarsely ground malt, makes it into large loaves of a sourdough bread, lets it rise, and bakes it very slightly, so that only the outer crust becomes bread and all the inside remains dough. These loaves are then broken apart, thrown into a large pot of water, and allowed to ferment. The resulting beer is called "bouzah." You will recognize this bread stage as a mashing process, where the elevated temperature stimulates the enzyme activity of saccharification, producing the sugar necessary for alcoholic fermentation.

Just as historians of Assyrian and ancient Egyptian beer technology keep referring to bread beers, so also the New England records point to bread as a source of homemade beers. Some of our records appear to be quite inaccurate. John Winthrop was missing something when he wrote about American beers to the Royal Society of London in 1662 that "Beere out of Bread . . . is found to be as well Coloured, and as pleasant, and every way as good and very wholesome without any windy Quality, and keepeth better from Souring then any other Beere . . . therefore that way of Brewing is most in use in that Country, that way of Maulting being also yet little knowne."

If you follow his recipe ("of makeing Beere, of Bread, is onely by makeing the Bread . . . and then breake it or Cutt it into greate Lumps, as bigg as a mans Fist or bigger . . . then Mash it and proceed every way about brewing of it, as is used in Brewing Beere of Mault, adding hopps to it as to make Beere"), you will produce a rather unpleasant drink that is only slightly alcoholic (2 percent). This is certainly not alcoholic enough to enhance its keeping qualities, because of the lack of sugar in the wort. I suspect that his "bread making" should have been called a substitute for mashing, not for malting. Not being sufficiently conversant with beer making, he did not get it right.

Good beer can be made by the bread-making method, however, and in many ways it is a surer way of mashing than the water-bath method described earlier. Remember that the early settlers never used a thermometer. They adjusted the mashing temperature of the malt in water by taste—too hot if they tasted the acetic acid, too cold if it did not taste sweet—and for a six-hour mash over a wood-burning stove this was hard to do. (The bread method substituted a visual indicator for the taste indicator.) The bread needed to rise in the oven to its maximum height but should not turn brown or the enzyme action would be stopped. The actual total time that it took the farm wife was several hours with either method. Even though the time over the fire was much less, hence probably easier to control, the bread had to be mixed, kneaded, and left to rise twice before it was put into the oven for its light bake.

Stretching the malt with other cereals was simple to do in the bread-making process. Corn meal, rye, and wheat flours were all used to save malt. The early settlers also used flour made from nuts to add food value to their breads. Particularly common were chestnuts and acorns. Chestnuts could be used directly and were dried and ground just as they fell from the trees. Acorns, although they were a very common food, had to be washed of their very bitter tannic acid. Whether or not the settlers brought with them the knowledge of how to treat acorns is not clear, but they certainly could have learned it from the Indians, who ate large quantities of acorns. The Indian technique was to shell the acorns in the fall, pound them to a coarse pulp which they put in woven baskets in a running stream, and let the nuts rinse for several weeks until sweet to the taste.

## Modern Equivalents

There is nothing special about the bread making for beer except that you must use malt flour, which you will probably have to grind for yourself. Any bread recipe will do. The one I find most successful is the following:

*Scald 2 cups of milk;*
*In ¼ cup warm water (110°F) dissolve 1 pkg. yeast;*
*When milk is cooled to 110° add water and yeast;*
*Add:*
> *2 tablespoons sugar or molasses*
> *2 teaspoons salt*
> *2 tablespoons of melted butter or Wesson oil*

*Stir*
*Gradually add 4 cups flour*
*Stir vigorously*
*Stir in another 1½ cups flour;*
*Knead in ½ cup or more flour until dough is elastic and not sticky. This should take about 10 minutes.*
*Grease bowl lightly, put in dough turned over once, cover with moist towel, and put out of draft at 85°F for about 1½ hrs. or until doubled in bulk.*
*Punch down in the middle, take out of the bowl, and knead a little.*
*Divide into two and flatten each half so that it is as long as the bread pan; roll it up sideways; turn under the ends; pinch seams; put in greased bread pan; cover.*
*Let it rise again for 1–1½ hours.*
*Bake at 300°F for about 20 minutes. Do not let it get brown.*
*After the bread is cool, break it into chunks and follow the instructions for brewing.*

The proportions of other flours which can be mixed with the malt flour are arbitrary. One third white flour will not have any effect on either the strength or the taste of the beer. One third corn or chestnut flour will be noticeable, but not a strong taste. One quarter acorn flour will give a very distinct nutty flavor to the beer. You can, of course, use the same recipe for making ordinary bread, although I would not waste malt flour for that purpose. If you are making bread to eat, bake at 375°F for 45 minutes.

About the nut flours: Chestnut flour is sold commercially in some specialty stores. If you grind your own, shell the nuts, dry them in a slow oven, grind coarsely, and dry again before making a fine-grind flour. Be sure *not* to use horse chestnuts—they are no relation and are poisonous.

If you try the Indian method of curing acorns, shell them, and grind them coarsely through a meat grinder. Tie them up in cheesecloth bags with a stone in each bag so that it will sink. Attach the bags with long strings to a tree or bush and throw them into a running brook. It takes about three weeks or a month to get the tannic acid out by this method. A quicker way is to boil the shelled kernels for a few hours, changing the water every time it gets to be the color of strong tea. After either method, dry the acorns as suggested for chestnuts. It takes five pounds of fresh acorns to make one cup of acorn flour.

# Brewing

The next process is that of boiling the liquor containing the extracted malt sugar with hops for several hours. It is called "brewing." It was at this point that the liquor was unknowingly sterilized and beer was made safe and healthful even with contaminated water.

It is impossible to know in the history of the development of beer whether hops were added because people liked its bitter taste and subsequently discovered it had great preservative qualities, or the reverse, but whichever way, it was early discovered in Europe that brewing the malted barley with hops helped to keep the beer from spoiling. This process had been introduced into England in the fifteenth century. Because most of the beer that was drunk in the early days was small beer, because of its lack of sugar, it was highly hopped to increase its preservation. The taste therefore was quite bitter, but being a familiar one it was the accepted flavor. For this reason even strong beer was much more heavily hopped than what we are used to in modern beers, and one can draw the general conclusion that the old beers were much more bitter than current tastes would accept.

It is unclear whether hops were indigenous to New England. We do know that the early pioneers did not find the vines in their early explorations around their settlements, and records show that the Massachusetts Bay Company ordered hop seeds from England in March 1629. The hop cones used in the beer brewing were not the only part of the plant that the farmers found useful. It was a common vine in the settler's kitchen garden. The young shoots in the spring were eaten as a special treat in salads (and can still be found in European markets), a wax extracted from the tendrils was used as a reddish-brown vegetable dye, the fibers were used in textiles as a substitute for flax, the stalks were used for basket and wicker-work, and the leaves and spent hops were an especially excellent food for sheep.

Because of their usefulness, hop vines were so commonly culti-vated that nowadays they often signal the location of long-aban-doned farms. Hop vines are bisexual, and only the seedless female catkins are good for beer. The male seedy hop blooms are very bitter. The taste we associate with hops is in the fine yellow resi-nous powder found on the surface of the cones, called "lupulin."

Although present day nomenclature does not signify it, origi-nally "ale" was not hopped and "beer" was. Ale was therefore frag-ile and had to be drunk soon after it was made, while beer could be stored and aged in barrels for months.

Hops contain tannin, which helps to clear the beer, oils which provide the flavor, and resins which act as the preservative. Most of the flavor was lost in the prolonged boiling necessary to extract the resins. To get around this, old recipes often suggest that part of the hops be kept back until the last five minutes or so of the boil-ing time. Another method was called "dry hopping": a quantity of the dried hops was added directly to the finished beer as it was put into its storage barrel, and the hops flavor was infused as part of the ageing process. In taverns the casks were set up on a stillage and the beer was drawn off by a tap so that the hops remained undisturbed while the beer was used. When various pumping de-vices were employed, the hops could get drawn up into the beer, spoiling its appearance and also causing blockages. So with the modernization of beer-dispensing methods, dry hopping has fallen into disuse.

*Hops*

# Do It Yourself

If you use commercial malt syrup, you do not have to brew it. On the other hand, if you have mashed malt cereal, add 1 ounce of dried hops (it comes both in bulk or in compressed cakes) to the liquor from two pounds of malt cereal and boil for three hours. Add two or three tablespoonfuls of the hops in the last ten minutes of boiling, or try dry hopping. After the brewing is completed, the spent hops should be strained out. The resulting liquid is called the "wort" and is ready for fermenting.

Rather than buy dried hops, you may want to find your own vines. They often grow along old roads and around ruined cellar holes. If you know what you are looking for, they are easy enough to spot by the cones or catkins, illustrated in the accompanying sketch. It is only in the fall, in cone time, that it is practical to find the vines, because you must identify their sex. Take the cones apart and look for the seeds. Only the female seedless ones should be used. Gather the cones and let them dry, then pull them apart to produce a flaky pile. One ounce of dry hops has a volume of one quart dry measure.

# Ground Ivy

Gill-over-the-ground, cat's foot, robin-in-the-hedge, alehoof, ale-cost, alehove, field balm, and ground ivy are all names for the common weed that was very often used to give the bitter taste to beer. The name "gill" is said to come from the French *guille*, to ferment, and the word "ale" appears in three of these names, attesting to the usefulness of this little plant. Actually many other bitter plants were also used in the steeping of beer, including sweet mary, tansy, sage, wormwood, and sweet gale, but ground ivy was the most common after hops, since it, too, has preservative qualities.

The ground ivy was gathered in the late summer when the leaves were fully developed (see sketch). When the leaves were thoroughly dried, they were separated from the stalks and used in the same manner as dried hops.

*Ground Ivy*

# Try It

It takes one half a peck of fresh plants to make an ounce of dried leaves. Gathering them is easy, since you can usually find a lush patch where you can reach down and pull up the plants by the handful. They break off easily from their roots so that what you get is clean. Separating the dried leaves from the runners is much more time consuming (and boring). Allow yourself several hours to pick over your dried weeds to get the one ounce of leaves you need for a ground ivy substitute for hops in the standard beer recipe.

If you use canned malt syrup, you can boil it with ground ivy to try the taste. Use the plain (not the hop-flavored) malt for this.

# Spruce Beer

One of the favorite beers in the seventeenth and eighteenth centuries was spruce beer. The early settlers prized it as a protection against scurvy, and it was discovered very early the "essence" of spruce could replace hops as a preservative for beer. Farmers made spruce beer in the spring from the fresh shoots of the black or red spruce, in the same way as any other beer, merely by replacing fresh spruce shoots for dried hops.

Not every type of spruce makes satisfactory beer, and recognizing the proper type is essential. The red and black spruce are very similar in general appearance to the hemlock, which is to be avoided. (It is not poisonous, however. The hemlock juice that Socrates drank was a completely different plant, an herb related to the carrot.) There are clear differences. The hemlock never grows on high mountain slopes, which is just where the red and black spruce thrive. The needles of the hemlock tend to be flat and have two silvery lines on their undersides, like the balsam fir, whereas these spruces have four-sided needles, bright green for the red and bluish green for the black. The distinguishing characteristic in the spring comes from the cones. The small egg-shaped cones of the spruces often remain on the trees for several years, while the similar-looking cones of the hemlock always drop off during the winter.

"Essence of spruce" was a spruce extract. The green shoots were covered with water and boiled until the water was pungent, strongly flavored, and reddish brown. The liquid was strained off and boiled down to half of its original volume. It was then bottled for use all year around. There are many recipes for making this beer. Two famous ones were given by Benjamin Franklin (*Benjamin Franklin on the Art of Eating*, Princeton 1958, p. 57) and by Jeffrey Amherst (*The Journal of Jeffrey Amherst*, ed. J. C. Webster, Toronto 1931, p. 152).

*Hemlock*

# Do It

If you want to make spruce beer yourself, just a handful of black spruce shoots picked in the spring is sufficient. Use as you would hops. If you are making beer from commercial malt syrup, buy the non-hopped variety and add the handful of shoots to the fermenting wort. If you cannot find the proper kind of fresh spruce shoots, you can buy "oil of spruce" or "spruce extract" from nature food stores. Use two ounces of this for five gallons of spruce beer.

*Spruce*

# Ginger Beer

The use of ginger as a spice is one of the oldest on record. The Greeks are known to have imported it from southern Arabia, and the Romans brought it to Britain when they settled on that island. Ginger was not only valued for its strong taste as a seasoning but was widely used as a medicine for stomach disorders. The early settlers brought it with them from England. Ginger root (it is really a rhizome) was one of the main spice imports from Jamaica both to England and to the colonies, and it is not surprising that it was used instead of hops in making beer. The rhizomes keep well, and a little can go a long way.

There were times in the country's history before the introduction of lager beer when the commercial sale of ginger beer exceeded both hopped beer or cider.

## Try It

Crush two ounces of ginger root, put it in a gallon or so of water and boil for an hour. Strain out the root pulp and use the ginger water as part of the liquid in the standard beer recipe. Use unhopped malt to get the full effect of the ginger taste, since it is a fairly subtle additive.

## Fermentation

Yeast is a living organism which is classified with the fungi because it contains no chlorophyll and cannot therefore make its own food supply from carbon dioxide and water as do green plants. Yeasts are present in the bloom of fruits, in the nectar of flowers, on grains and seeds, and to a lesser extent in the soil and floating in the air. They are a single-cell form of life, invisible to the naked eye. They reproduce themselves by growing a bud which grows until it is identical with the parent cell and then detaches itself. Each yeast cell can on the average produce about 30 daughter cells before it is exhausted and dies.

Yeasts have evolved fermentation as a means of producing the energy necessary for their growth and reproduction in the absence of oxygen. Alcoholic fermentation will take place in either the presence or the absence of oxygen, but the amount of alcohol produced from a given supply of sugar decreases as the oxygen supply increases. The reason is that when plenty of oxygen is available, for example in bread making, the yeast can oxidize a considerable proportion of the sugar completely to carbon dioxide and water, and in

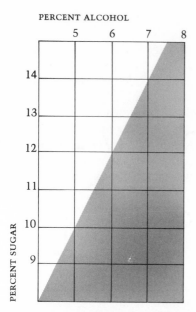

PERCENT ALCOHOL

*The More Sugar, The More Alcohol*

this way it obtains a great deal more energy for its growth than would be provided by fermentation alone.

In fermenting beer it is desirable that a thriving colony of yeast be built up in the shortest possible time, but once this stage is reached, the supply of oxygen must be cut off so that the maximum amount of alcohol is formed from the sugar in the wort. These conditions are almost automatically present in normal beer-making procedures. During its preparation, the wort is aerated to a greater or lesser extent by stirring and pouring it into the fermentation vessel, and an air space is usually left above the surface of the liquid. The yeast uses this oxygen for the initial phases of its growth. By the time the supply is exhausted, the original yeast colony has grown large enough to maintain a satisfactory rate of fermentation throughout the whole body of the liquid. Yeast will usually continue to ferment the liquid either until it exhausts the sugar present or until it is inhibited from further activity by the amount of alcohol which is formed. The alcohol does not kill the yeast but forces it into a dormant state.

Yeasts are perishable organisms, however, and the early settlers had no refrigeration and no knowledge of how to dry yeasts to preserve their potency. This dictated to a considerable degree their beer-making schedules. As long as malt was available, beer-making from the lees of a previous batch was a continuous process, since there was always enough good yeast left in the lees. Also, beer could be made from the yeast or sourdough used in the bread making that was also a fairly continuous process in the country kitchens. The amount of beer being made was therefore dictated by the rate at which the family consumed it.

Baker's yeast induces a vigorous frothy fermentation that is usually of comparatively short duration, after which the dead and inhibited cells slowly settle to the bottom to form a rather loose and easily disturbed deposit. Clarification is therefore a slow process. This type of yeast has the advantage of fermenting at comparatively low temperatures, and the alcohol tolerance is acceptably high, running around 12–14 percent alcohol. If the yeast was used for beer, it took on a strong smell because of the presence of hop residues, and such yeast was reserved for brewing beer alone.

Sourdough, the leavening agent used to "enliven the whole" by the early pioneers, is a simple combination of whole milk and flour kept in a warm place until it begins to ferment from the activity of the wild yeast in the flour and to some extent in the milk. When ready it is not a very appealing sight, and we can only admire the ancient Egyptians, to whom the first use is attributed, for their courage and sense of adventure in recognizing the potential of this gooey mass with its slightly offensive smell! Since the wild yeasts in the flour and milk were being relied on, the process did not always work, but once sourdough was started, it was kept going by replacing equal parts of milk and flour. It was used for both bread and beer.

A modern attempt to make sourdough the way the early Americans did by just mixing flour and milk and waiting for the yeasts to grow will not be successful if the ingredients are bought from a store. First of all the pasteurization of the milk will destroy any live airborne yeasts that might be available to grow. Just as important is that modern flours have been stripped of the wheat germ that provided the enzymes to turn the wheat starch into the sugar necessary for yeast growth. The germ is a little sack that forms about 3 percent of the kernel volume and lies along the opposite side from the crease on the wheat kernel. It is the embryo or sprouting tissue of the seed. In modern flour production it is separated from the kernel before milling, because it contains an oil that limits the keeping quality of the flour. In colonial days, the farmers either milled their own flour as they needed it or went often to the miller, for the flour kept poorly. For making sourdough, they could easily use a hand mill in the kitchen to provide the small quantity necessary.

With our present knowledge of the fermentation process we can see that experience had taught the farmers how to maximize their chances of success. Their technique was to pour the wort, after it had cooled down from the brewing process, into a barrel, "pitch in" the yeast—often the lees from a former batch of sourdough if they were starting from scratch—and with the bung hole uncovered would wait until the violent foaming fermentation had subsided (a matter of only a day or so). This was, of course, to build up the yeast colony in the presence of some oxygen. The bung was then laid loosely into the bung hole and the whole was allowed to sit in a reasonably warm place until the fermentation was over and the barrel was no longer "singing." This might take a few weeks, with the loosely plugged barrel keeping the ullage full of carbon dioxide to the exclusion of oxygen to assure a good alcoholic fermentation.

Often the beer was drunk as soon as fermentation ceased. If it was to be stored, it would be transferred out of the fermentation barrel, a process called "racking," into a storage barrel, which was filled to the very top and the bung hammered into the hole.

# Basic Recipe

Start your beer making with a type that is the closest to the commercial beer with which you are familiar. In terms of the old colonial beers this will be a "strong" beer typical of what gentlemen and the aristocracy drank who could afford paying for sugar imported from the West Indies and malt imported from England.

Bring one gallon of water to the boiling point, remove from the stove to keep from burning the malt, and add one three-pound can of hop-flavored malt syrup. Dissolve completely. Fermentation is most easily done in a five-gallon carboy. Put a little cold water in the bottom of the carboy to keep it from cracking and pour in the dissolved malt syrup and water. Dissolve six cups of sugar in warm water and add this to the carboy. All our modern ingredients are so purified that they may not naturally give a foamy beer; if you want a foamy beer, add one quarter of a cup of rice. Now fill the carboy with water up to about the place where it starts to neck in, adjusting the temperature so that when the jug is full, it will be lukewarm. Add one package of dried yeast.

Leave the carboy uncovered at room temperature for about 24 hours. By then it should be fermenting actively, with the foam tending almost to overflow the neck. (This is why you did not fill the container all the way.) Now seal the wort with a "water seal" or "fermentation lock." There are many different types, simple and fancy, all designed to let the $CO_2$ out and not let any oxygen from the air in. A survey of the different types is shown in the sketch. Let the fermentation proceed until it is almost finished. You can judge the "almost" in a number of ways; the advantage of fermenting in a glass carboy is that you can see what is happening. You can see the $CO_2$ bubbles coming up through the wort; and when these have almost ceased, the beer is ready for bottling. Another way to tell when you have reached "almost" is by timing the bubbles that come out through the fermentation lock. When the lock is bubbling at a rate of less than one bubble per minute, the fermentation is "almost" completed. Experience can teach you another way, but until you have done it a few times, it is not easy to pick the right point. The wort is a light brown, very cloudy color when it is actively fermenting; but as it nears completion, it gets darker and clearer. When the dark clear part of the wort fills about half of the carboy, the beer is ready for bottling.

The one bubble a minute rule is an average and depends some-

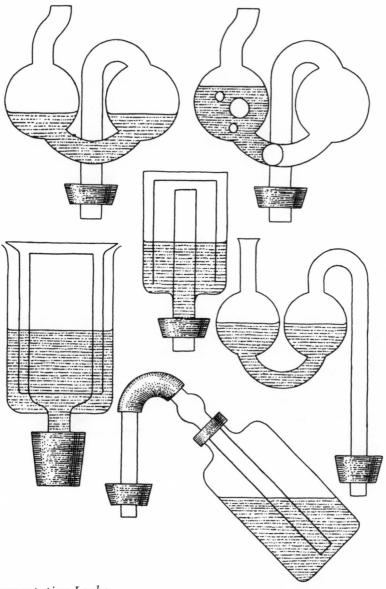

*Fermentation Locks*

what on the room temperature where the fermentation is carried out. If the beer turns out very frothy or yeasty, lengthen the fermentation time; if it tends to be "still," shorten the time before you bottle it.

The beer is now ready to be siphoned into bottles. Further fermentation in the bottles will provide the carbonation to make an acceptable modern beer. One teaspoon of sugar per quart bottle or one half teaspoon per twelve-ounce bottle will be the proper amount. Put the sugar in the bottle before siphoning the beer. This is called "priming". Cap the bottles with a crimp top. Shake up the bottles to dissolve all the sugar. Let them sit in a warm place for a week, and then move them to a cool place for storage. Do not drink for three weeks to a month.

Modern beer standards require that beer be clear. This beer will be clear in the bottle, but the lees are easily disturbed, and if you want to maintain the clarity, decant into a pitcher with one continuous motion, watching to stop when the lees start to pour with the liquid. You will thereby lose about one quarter of an inch of the content in a quart bottle.

Another way to get clear beer is to use champagne bottles with hollow plastic stoppers. Store the bottles upside down during the priming fermentation. The lees will collect inside the stopper. Keeping the bottle always upside down, remove the stopper with the neck of the bottle under water. Put your thumb over the mouth of the bottle as soon as you have withdrawn the stopper, lift it out of the water, turn it right side up, and cap it immediately. If you chill the beer before you carry out this operation, more of the $CO_2$ will be dissolved in the beer and you will lose less fizz.

# Variations

Based on the basic beer recipe, which simulates *strong beer* (about 8 percent alcohol), you can recreate many of the old New England beers with the following modifications of the basic recipe.

(a) It is more authentic to leave out the priming and have still beer. Also, you should drink it at room temperature—the farmers had no ice. Furthermore, you should not decant it. Even shake it up a little. The colonials knew that there was nutritional value in the spent yeast.

(b) *Small beer,* or *single beer:* Use the same procedure but add no sugar either in the fermenting or the priming stage. Small beer was weak (4–5 percent alcohol) and still. Small beer was not aged. This was the most common of all the colonial American beers.

(c) *Middle beer, ships beer,* or *table beer:* Use only three cups of sugar in the fermentation stage.

(d) If you could have afforded molasses (imported from the West Indies), you could have had many dark beers. Substitute the same number of cups of molasses as the recipe calls for cups of sugar. Three cups molasses + three cups sugar will make dark; six cups molasses will make very dark; "black strap" molasses will make black beer.

(e) Substitute plain malt syrup for the hops-flavored kind and you will make old-fashioned ale.

(f) If you want to taste beer made with malt stretched with corn without carrying out the mashing process yourself, you can buy "Extract of Malted Barley & Corn, Hop-Flavored." Use a three-pound can of this instead of the basic recipe for hop-flavored malt syrup.

(g) *Home brewed:* If you want to start from malted barley, the instructions given under "Modern Equivalents" for mashing and brewing are for the same five gallons we have been considering here. The wort thus produced is equivalent to the malt syrup dissolved in water and all the same directions apply.

(h) *Sourdough yeast:* The standard modern equivalent recipe suggests that you "add one package of dried yeast." You may replace this with one tablespoon of sourdough. After this has been done, refill the sourdough container with flour and milk to keep the sourdough coming.

# CHAPTER FOUR

# Apples and Ciders

Next to beer, and in fact sometimes rivaling it, apple cider was the most common drink among the Colonial Americans. Apple trees were not native to the American continent but were brought to Massachusetts nine years after the arrival of the first Pilgrims and probably into northern New England in the early seventeenth century by Jesuits from Canada. From there the trees soon escaped into the wilderness, spread by the birds and the wild animals, so that by the time the settlers started to push back the New England frontier and to carve out their farms with axes and plows, apple trees were to be found all through the forests.

Apple trees do not grow true to seed. There is no relationship between the kind of apple that a tree produces and the seed from which it sprouts. It has been estimated that there is only one chance in 10,000 that a really good apple of any sort will result from an apple tree grown from a seed. Thus all named apple trees are propagated by grafting.

I have never known anyone who could really enjoy eating a wild apple, but clearly I have never known a person like Henry Thoreau who wrote in his essay on Wild Apples:

*Here on this rugged and woody hillside has grown an appletree, not planted by man, no relic of a former orchard, but a natural growth, like the pines and oaks . . . Who knows but this chance wild fruit, planted by a cow or a bird on some remote and rocky hillside, where it is as yet unobserved by man, may be the choicest of all its kind, and foreign potentates shall hear of it, and royal societies seek to propagate it, though the virtues of the perhaps truly crabbed owner of the soil may never be heard of—at least beyond the limits of his village? It was thus the FORTER and the BALDWIN grew.*

*Every wild apple shrub excites our expectation thus, somewhat
as every wild child. It is perhaps a prince in disguise . . . There is
. . . about all natural products a certain volatile and ethereal quality which cannot be vulgarized, or bought and sold . . .*

*I frequently pluck wild apples of so rich and spicy a flavor that I
wonder all orchardists do not get a scion from the tree, and I fail
not to bring home my pockets full. But perchance, when I take
one out of my desk and taste it in my chamber I find it unexpect-
edly crude,—sour enough to set a squirrel's teeth on edge and
make a jay scream . . .*

*I fear that he who walks over these fields a century hence will
not know the pleasure of knocking off wild apples. Ah, poor man,
there are many pleasures which he will not know!*

The first apple orchard in New England was planted on Beacon
Hill, Boston, with trees brought from England by an eccentric cler-
gyman named William Blaxton some time before 1625. People
made so much fun of Rev. Blaxton because he trained a bull to the
saddle and went around distributing apples and flowers to his
neighbors from the bull's back that in 1635 he moved to Study Hill
near Pawtucket, Rhode Island, to continue his apple cultivation.
There he developed what he called a Yellow Sweeting, later called
the Sweet Rhode Island Greening. It was probably the first named
apple to originate in America. This is not to be confused with the
Rhode Island Greening which originated near Newport in 1748
from seed planted by a tavern keeper named Green who had a side
business of growing apple trees from seed. Green's tree was so popular that it was said that the tree was killed in a very few years by
excessive cutting of scions that were taken to every northern
colony.

Not only did farmers plant apple seeds to see what would come
up, but many people searched the woods and forests for good apples
from which to make cider, the apple's principal use. Among the
early discoveries was the Roxbury Russet found near Roxbury,
Massachusetts, in 1649.

One of the most famous New England apples was found by
Loammi Baldwin of Woburn, Massachusetts. The story is told in

Samuel Sewall's *History of Woburn*. It is said to have happened in 1784.

*As Col. Baldwin was one day surveying land at a place called Butters' Row in Wilmington, near the bound of that town, Woburn and Burlington, he observed one or more woodpeckers continually flying to a certain tree, growing on land of Mr. James Butters, hard by. Prompted by curiosity to ascertain the cause of their frequenting that tree, he at length went to it; and finding under it apples of an excellent flavor, and well worth cultivating, he returned to the tree the next spring, and took from it scions to graft into stocks of his own. Other persons in that vicinity, induced by his example or advice, grafted trees of theirs soon after with scions from the same stock. And, subsequently, whenever Col. Baldwin attended court, or went into different parts of the country, as High Sheriff, he was accustomed to carry scions of this variety of apple with him, and to distribute them among his friends; so that this species of fruit soon came to be extensively known and cultivated. The original tree, it is said, was blown down in the famous "September gale" in 1815.*

*At first, apples of this description were called by many, "Butters' Apples," from the name of the person upon whose land the original tree was found; and by others "Woodpecker Apples," from the bird, whose constant flight to it attracted the notice of Col. Baldwin, and led to the discovery of the excellency of the fruit which grew on it. But, on a certain day, (it is reported) when Col. Baldwin had a party of gentlemen at his house to dine, he set before them a dish of these apples; and one of his guests, admiring their good qualities, asked him by what name they were known? "By no name in particular," the Colonel replied; "call them, if you please, Baldwin apples.*

Another apple that is still popular today was found growing wild by John McIntosh in 1796 near the St. Lawrence River in Dundas County, Ontario. He named it the McIntosh Red.

There were hundreds of old apples, but faced with the desire to reproduce the taste of old New England cider you have a problem in finding colonial apples since most of the old varieties were systematically destroyed during the depression years of the 1930's. During those years the Works Progress Administration was set up by the Federal Government to provide jobs for many unemployed men and women. At the suggestion of the Massachusetts Fruit Growers Association one of the projects adopted was to seek out and destroy all old abandoned apple trees as a way of reducing the serious insect and disease problems that were plaguing the fruit industry. Most of the old varieties were thus lost forever. Among the apples that did survive this program and were used for cider in New England before 1800 are the following:

**Baldwin** or **Woodpecker.** Wilmington, Massachusetts, 1740.
**Fameuse** or **Snow.** This is one of the oldest varieties grown on this continent. It was imported from France and was particularly popular in the northern colonies.
**High Top Sweet.** Its origin is unknown but it was a great favorite with the Plymouth Colony.
**Lady.** Its origin was in France before 1600.
**McIntosh Red.** Ontario, 1796, a seedling from a fameuse.
**Ribston.** It came from Yorkshire, England, around 1700.
**Rhode Island Greening.** Near Newport, Rhode Island, about 1700.
**Roxbury Russet.** Roxbury, Massachusetts, 1649.
**Sop of Wine.** Imported from England very early
**Westfield-Seek-No-Further.** Westfield, Massachusetts, 1750.
**Williams** or **Ladys.** Roxbury, Massachusetts, 1760.

If you want to taste old New England cider you must graft trees from scions of these varieties or get some from one who has.

The techniques of grafting have been known since the days of the ancient Greeks and the method used most by the colonists is known as cleft grafting. It is illustrated by the accompanying sketches. A root stock tree was sawed off, split down the middle, and two scions inserted. The early farmers had a special tool, also shown. The broad blade was used to split the trunk and the wedge at the end kept the wood apart as the scions were being inserted.

The scions were whittled to long thin wedges. Usually they were the "suckers" or the straight unbranching year-old shoots that grow on the upper sides of mature branches of the desired kind of tree. Ideally they were fresh cut. With the typical resilience that apple trees show, however, a remarkable percentage of them seem to survive long journeys wrapped in damp rags to keep them moist. Two scions are customarily inserted, to make full use of the cambium layer (between the wood and the bark).

After a year or so, when all is growing vigorously, one of the shoots is cut off and the bark heals over the wound. To keep the cut parts from drying out, a grafting wax is smeared over all the exposed parts. The early settlers used beeswax for this, but because it was so soft, particularly in the hot sun, it had to be reapplied several times a year. By the early part of the nineteenth century a regular grafting wax was stocked in country stores throughout New England that was considerably harder and would not melt off.

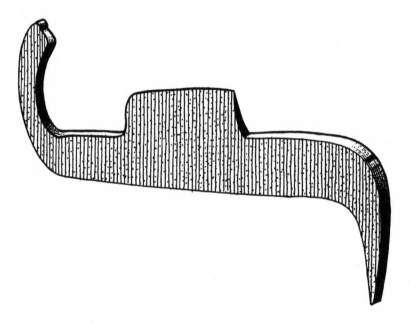

*Grafting Tool*

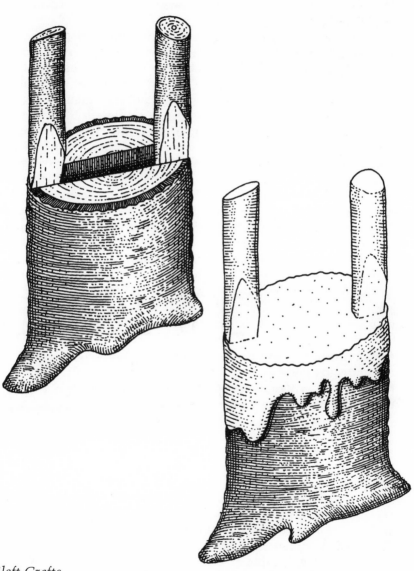

*Cleft Grafts*

This consisted of two parts rosin, one part beeswax, and one half part linseed oil.

The shapes of apple trees are easily controlled by pruning, and farmers usually cut out the center branches of the trees to get better sunlight on the inner fruit. They also keep the trees from growing tall so that the apples may be harvested more easily. Although apple trees can grow all over New England, the extended cold for many months in extreme northern sections did affect the vigor of the trees and delayed the ripening of the fruit. Here an ambitious farmer would "ground prune" his trees. Ground pruning is still practiced in Siberia, and we do not know whether this technique was brought over from Russia by immigrants from there or whether it was rediscovered by the New England colonists. It consisted of never letting the trees grow more than about two feet off the ground. The original cleft graft was made as close to the ground as possible; the side branches of the scions were allowed to grow, but not the vertical leader. As the horizontal branches tended to arch upward toward the sky light, they were pinned down to the ground to train them outward instead. The purpose of this was to keep the entire tree close to the ground so that during the very cold weather it was entirely buried under the snow and thus protected from the extremes of wind and weather. The trees bear just as well when pruned thus, but it was of course a lot more work to keep the trees growing horizontally, and each tree took up a lot more space. Nevertheless, where the weather dictated, it was used to get a better crop.

# Advice to Moderns

As might be expected, the taste of cider depends on the type of apple used, so that if you want to recreate old ciders, you have to use the proper apples. Some old-type apples such as Baldwins are still available commercially, but it is really better if you can grow your own. Very few nurseries can supply any old-fashioned apple trees, so you will almost certainly have to graft if you want to expand your ciders beyond the few types available on the market.

One can graft onto any kind of apple stock, either an established old tree or a wild seedling. The former is easier, but the latter is more fun. Seedlings are always coming up around apple trees. They should be dug up in the early spring when they are about two years old. If you are starting an orchard, the spacing between the trees should be not less than 40 feet. Let a transplanted seedling get established before attempting a graft. The young tree should be about an inch in diameter at its base before it is used as stock for cleft grafting.

Grafting is very straightforward. The previous sketch illustrates the technique. The root-stock trunk or limb should be cut off with a fine-toothed saw so as not to injure the bark any more than necessary. If the graft is being made on root-stock, cut off the young tree close to the ground. You do not have to use a grafting tool as illustrated; an ordinary wood chisel will serve. You can buy grafting wax, or grafting "compound" as it is often called, at farmers' supply houses.

Graft in the early spring just as the trees are starting their leaf buds. Suckers make excellent scions. After the grafts have grown for two years, cut off the less vigorous scion close to the main bark and paint the wound with tree-paint so that the cut will heal over. The graft should start bearing in about five years. You may graft as many different kinds of apple on a single tree as you want, but it takes about one bushel of apples to make a gallon of cider, so if you want to taste different kinds of ciders you have to have enough apples of a given type to make a varietal cider.

A farm that has been in one family for several generations is a likely source of scions from old-fashioned types and in general farmers are complimented to be asked for scions from their favorite trees. Also, the Worcester (Mass.) County Horticultural Society operates a "preservation orchard" next to the Old Sturbridge folk museum. They have a large collection of old variety apple trees and will supply scions from these trees to those interested.

# Pests

In the early days when the farms were small and isolated, pests on the apples and the apple trees apparently were not a serious problems At least there is little evidence that worms and blights bothered either the quality or the quantity of the cider crop. There were some blights, however, and the early farmers took two steps to control them. They used to hang "moth traps" on the trees. These were open cups made of birch bark or the shells of small gourds filled with various attractive sticky mixtures. One common recipe was two thirds molasses, one third corn syrup diluted to six times its volume with water. Five or six cups of this mixture per tree were reasonably effective at controlling the pests in their flying stage. With a small farm, chickens, pigs, and horses were kept under the trees to eat up the apple drops and thereby reduce the reinfestation from wormy fruit. As the farms got larger, the apple maggot (called by the late nineteenth century New England farmers the "railroad worm" because its marking is like the ties of a railroad track) became a real pest.

Apple maggots live in the ground from late fall until the following July, and a small percentage of them can live over to a second year. The farmers discovered that they could control this pest by burying the drops and the pomace under at least a foot of hard-packed earth to prevent the flies from emerging. Three pomace pits were used in rotation. Each year's waste was kept underground in one pit for two years. The third pit was cleaned out during the summer and the three-year rotted pomace used as good compost. This third-year pit was then filled with fresh wormy apples and the pomace from the press in the fall, to be buried before the flies matured in the following summer.

# Modern Equivalents

Apple pests are a real problem in New England now. So many orchards and apple trees have been left uncared for that it is rare to see an untended tree producing sound apples. Most people who want good apples undertake an extensive chemical spray program. If you want to do this, your county agent or local farm bureau can advise you as to what to use.

If your trees are somewhat isolated—outside the flying range of flies and moths from other apple trees—try the moth trap and pomace pit methods. A pit three feet deep and two feet across (remember that you need three of these eventually) will take care of thirty bushels of apples and pomace. The apple residues rot down a surprising amount, and if at the end of the apple season the pit is overfull by a foot or more, don't worry. By the end of the winter it will be below ground level and for the next year or so you will have to add earth on top to make sure that people don't fall into the hole.

Do not neglect to pick the last of the crop before a hard frost sets in. Everyone wants to stretch out the cider season as long as possible. However, if you leave apples on the trees too long, they get frozen and will not feed through your cider press properly. Early apples all fall off the trees long before frost, but good late maturing cider apples can often get left undropped. Sooner or later you absolutely must pick every last apple off the trees whether it is good or bad. Put the good ones to cider and the bad ones in the pomace pit. If you don't, you are asking for trouble in reinfecting next year's crop.

It is worth noting in passing that worm-free apples are essential for pies or applesauce, but for cider the worms make no difference if you are using a hand press. A hand press does not put enough pressure on the apples to squash the worms and the pomace acts as a filter.

# Sweet Cider

Apple cider is as typical a New England drink as there is. In the old days every farm had at least a few apple trees in its side yard and almost always a cider press in the barn. Even the small villages had their cider "mills" sometimes before they had their general stores.

In making cider, fresh-picked apples were not usually used since the flavor improves by drying them for a few days. This was called "sweating" the apples, and used to be carried out by piling up the fruit in heaps on the ground and waiting until the fruit had lost about one tenth of its water content. This might take several days to a week depending upon the weather. The same thing could, of course, be accomplished by using the "drops" and letting them stay on the ground for a few days. However, if horses, cows, and pigs roamed the orchard or the countryside abounded in rabbits, squirrels, or game birds, the drops were soon badly damaged.

The process of cider-making involves three distinct steps: breaking up the apples, pressing out the juice, and ageing the juice into cider.

The most primitive technique was first to break the apples apart by pounding them with wooden mallets and then to press the juice out using what was called a "sweep" press ("sweep" as in well-sweep). These presses, when used by a whole community, could be of very large size. The crushed apples were laid out on a heavy wooden or stone platform equipped with juice channels to guide the liquid into a collecting bucket. On top of the pile of crushed apples was placed a heavy board. The sweep was a long heavy wooden pole tied down close to the platform to provide a large mechanical advantage to anyone pulling down on the other end. Pressing was accomplished first by the farmer using his own weight, and then by hanging a whole series of heavy rocks on the end to further increase the pressure until no more juice could be extracted.

One can still find some of these sweep presses in folk museums. The remains of what appears to be a most extensive sweep mill has become a tourist attraction in North Salem, New Hampshire. Under the title of "Mystery Hill" a commercial tourist group is telling the story of ancient religious zealots migrating from Europe long before the Vikings and setting up a sacrificial altar, blood grooves and all, and living in what for many years was known locally as Pattee's Caves. The "altar" stone has all the characteristics of the usual base plate of a cider press and the extensive fieldstone "caves" look like the many underground apple or root storage cellars that are still to be found throughout New England.

Breaking the apples with hand mallets was not satisfactory for making large amounts of cider, and communities would build a cider mill for this purpose. The apparatus consisted of a heavy mill-stone set up to roll on its rim in a circular channel on a long axle pivoted at the center of the channel circle. A long arm extended many feet beyond the stone pushed or pulled by men or teams of oxen or horses. After crushing, the pomace was moved to a press.

A convenient form of press was available as soon as a farmer could obtain a screw large enough to be used in a press. Hand cider presses have changed little for hundreds of years. They consist of two parts, a rotary crusher or grinder which drops the broken apples into a slotted cylindrical barrel, and a piston type screw press that squeezes out the juice. The usual home-farm type of cider press holds about a bushel of apples at a time.

After the juice has been expressed, it needs to be aged at room temperature for at least twenty-four hours before the apple juice turns to cider. Apple juice was used mainly for making jelly. Since fresh or "soft" cider does not keep long, it was drunk in the fall soon after it was pressed. It does freeze well, so that barrels left out in the cold weather provided some soft cider during the winter and on into the early spring, but most of it was allowed to ferment to what we now call "hard" cider, which the colonials just called "cider."

Understandably there was a considerable reluctance to let children drink too much strong drink. They were allowed, of course, to drink all the sweet cider they wanted, but this usually happened only during the late summer and early fall. Boiled fresh cider did not keep very well, particularly with the lack of understanding of cleanliness and sterilization. So it was not uncommon to make for the children what with time became only slightly alcoholic, but enough to improve its keeping qualities. The drink was called "ciderkin" or "water-cider" and was made by pouring water over the solid mash left after the cider had been pressed from the pomace. This was then put through the press again, and the expressed juice

was stored for the children. A rather tasteless drink, it was sometimes made more attractive by adding small amounts of molasses
and ginger.

## The Pomace

In the hard and rigorous life that the settlers had to endure, every
attempt was made not to waste anything. The squeezed pomace
was a useful by-product of cider making. Vinegar made from
pomace was a most important commodity for preserving, corning,
and pickling. The pomace was piled on a wooden platform and
allowed to ferment. In the course of a few days considerable heat
was evolved, and when the pile was warm to the touch, a pail or so
of warm water was poured over the pile to make up for the evapo-
ration. In a day or so more of it was put through the press again.
The expressed liquid was poured into open shallow pans set in a
warm room, often behind the stove, and in a few days good vinegar
resulted. This was then bottled and stored.

Apple brandy was also made from the ground-up apples by those
who wanted to take the trouble. After grinding, the apples were put
into a cask to ferment. We are told that to determine the progress
of the fermentation a stick was pushed into the center of the barrel, and if bubbling or hissing noises were heard when the stick
was pulled out, the mass was still fermenting. If no sound was
heard, the content was ready for the still. The product was called
"apple brandy" in distinction from the distillation of hard cider
which was called "apple spirits." Both of these were more alcoholic than "applejack," which is concentrated by freezing.

Often the waste pomace from the press was used as a stock feed
for horses, hogs, cattle, and sheep.

## Do It Yourself

Sweet cider as the early settlers made it differs in some respects
from modern commercial sweet cider. The principal technical dif-

ference is that in the hand press the ground apples are subjected to much less pressure than with the modern hydraulic presses and hence the cider contains much less of the taste of the skin than is present in commercial cider. Also, of course, hand presses produce much less juice. A hand press gives about one gallon per bushel of apples while two to two and one half gallons per bushel from a commercial press is usual. Another difference between commercial cider and the home-pressed variety is in the water content. In normal commercial operation about 10 to 20 percent of water is added. This is not to cheat the customer, but to speed the process. First the apples are liberally washed with water and enter the grinders soaking wet. Second, water is added to hasten the juice extraction. Added water increases the difference in osmotic pressure between the juice contained in the fruit's cell structure and the free liquid outside the cellular structure of the pulp, thereby increasing the yield of apple juice. This latter procedure can be accomplished in a hand press by just waiting, sometimes as long as an hour between crushing and pressing.

To make your own cider a press is essential, however. Although old ones are somewhat hard to find, many still exist in old farms where they are no longer used. New ones are also available commercially. A cider press differs from a wine press in two ways. A cider press must always have associated with it an apple crusher to grind up the fruit before it is pressed. Also the slats which let the juice out of the sides of the pressing bucket are further apart in an apple press than a grape press. The apple juice must run freely, since the apple chunks to be pressed are considerably larger than grapes. There are two types of cider presses commonly available in New England, the one-bucket and the two-bucket, both illustrated in the figure. The one-bucket press is usually somewhat larger, so that a greater quantity of apples can be pressed at one time, but with the two-bucket press the process can be almost continuous if more than one person is involved, in that the grinding into the first bucket can take place while the pressing is being done in the other.

To make cider, then, you must first grind the apples. The grinder is the part of the press where you feed in whole apples at the top and the pulp falls down into the pressing bucket. After the bucket

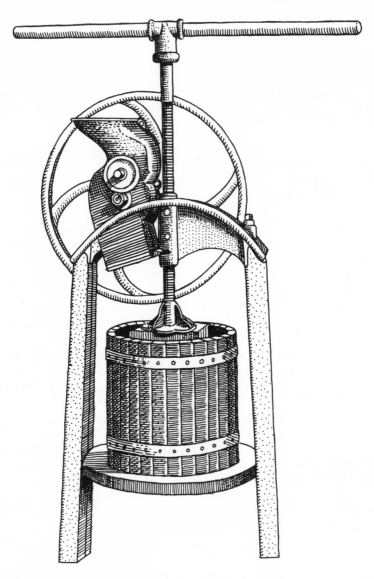

*Single Bucket Cider Press*

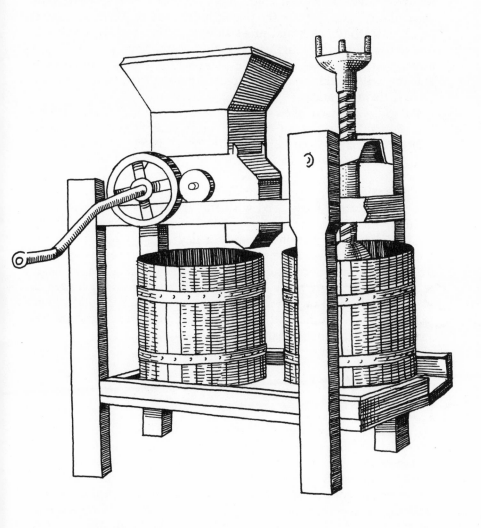

*Double Bucket Cider Press*

is full of pulp, let it stand for a quarter of an hour, or until the pulp takes on a golden brown color. This oxidation tends to break up the cell structure and lets the juice flow more freely. Put the piston block onto the bucket and press slowly so that the juice will run out without getting caught in the pulp. After you have pressed it down as hard as possible, let the press sit for a quarter of an hour and you will be able to turn the pressing screw still further, releasing a little more juice.

Put the expressed juice into jugs and store for at least twenty-four hours. What you get from the press is apple juice, not cider. Many New England farmers call this "fresh cider." If you want to keep it as apple juice, you must boil it to prevent it from turning into cider.

The ageing of apple juice into cider occurs spontaneously without the evolution of gas and with the accumulation of a grey deposit or "lees" on the bottom of the container. This is a rapid oxidation process, continuing only a day or so, which turns the apple juice into sweet cider. After this the cider can be separated from the lees by pouring off the liquid, or "decanting." When large amounts were being made, the sweet cider was initially stored in barrels fitted with a spigot or, as it was often called, a "spile," and drawn off into another barrel, usually for continued fermentation into hard cider. This transferring of the liquid, leaving behind the sludge at the bottom, was called "racking off."

# Hard Cider

Although the early colonists came with their beer and brought the knowledge of malting with them, their drinking habits soon changed from beer to cider. English grains did not thrive well during the first years of settlement before the tree stumps and roots rotted away enough so the fields could be properly plowed, and Indian corn seems to have resisted every attempt to produce a successful malt. Apple orchards were planted extensively, and in a few decades every prosperous farm had its apple orchard. Cider became plentiful and cheap. Roads were poor; markets for fresh fruits were lacking and essentially the entire crop of apples went into the manufacture of cider. This was not because apples were not good to eat. The fruit was widely used in the autumn, but the season was not long and the quantity necessary for this demand was not large. One good apple tree yields up to ten bushels of fruit and even a large family cannot eat many bushels.

Sweet cider keeps for less than a week at room temperature before it starts to ferment actively to hard cider. There are natural yeasts on the apples (the so-called "blush" on fresh apples), so that nothing needs to be added, and it is only toward the end of the fermentation that there was any risk of making vinegar instead of cider in case not enough $CO_2$ was being produced. In the violent part of the process, the "tumultuous" or "foaming" fermentation, the danger was only that the must might overflow the barrel. When the fermentation slowed down, the barrel was plugged with a loose bung or small sandbag. The soft hiss of the gas coming out around the edges was called the "singing of the cider." After the singing stopped, the farmer reduced the ullage (the empty space above the liquid) either by filling the barrel to overflowing with extra cider or by dropping stones into the barrel to raise the liquid level. The whole process took a month or two. In the spring the cider was racked off into storage barrels that were filled up right to the top, the bungs were driven in hard and the cider was aged for a couple of years before it was considered to be at its peak.

By our modern standards the hard cider that the early settlers drank was dry and not particularly alcoholic. The relation between the sugar content of the apples and the resulting strength of the cider is shown in graph 1, page 71.

There was a good deal of attention paid in the old literature to drinks for children. In the winter when milk was scarce, sweetened cider diluted with water was recommended as a beverage, sometimes warmed and with bread soaked in the mixture. When served cold and flavored with nutmeg, it seemed to be a popular summer drink.

If the farmers had honey or sugar to spare, addition of this to the sweet cider would, of course, increase the potency when fermented. During the eighteenth century, cider became an important export commodity from New England. To increase its alcoholic content and to improve its keeping quality, especially when shipped to hotter climates, sugar was often added. By the late eighteenth century the standard cider for sale in taverns ran around 7½ percent alcohol, the sugar content of the must having been raised from the 5 percent of the cider made from pure apples alone.

For those who could spare the sugar and who wanted to make a drink that was a little special, they produced what was often called "apple champagne." Some of the cider that was racked off in the spring was put directly into bottles with a teaspoon of sugar added—a process called "priming." The bottles were corked, the corks tied down, and the bottles put away in a dark corner of the cellar for a year or two. The added sugar contained the fermentation and provided a light natural carbonation to the finished cider.

# Try It

In the fall of the year some stands along the farm roads sell sweet cider that is unclarified and without any preservative added. This can be turned into hard cider with a minimum of effort. Five or ten gallon lots are good quantities to make at a time, although it is not necessary to press that much sweet cider at one time, since you can add subsequent amounts to the fermenting batch. Make or buy a suitable amount of sweet cider and put it in a carboy or barrel.

The fermentation uses up the sugar, so unless you prefer quite dry hard cider, add one cup of sugar, honey or maple syrup per gallon of sweet cider so that there will be some sweetness left over in the final liquor. Adding sugar up to a certain point will increase the alcoholic content of the finished cider, although if you add too much, the fermentation will be inhibited.

Add a cake or package of yeast. Seal with a fermentation lock and ferment to completion. This will take a month or so. Be careful not to fill the barrel too full, since this fermentation starts out violently and you can easily overflow your barrel. When the fermentation has ceased, siphon off the must from the lees into another barrel. Bung it lightly for a week to make sure that any fermentation that was stimulated by the racking will have stopped, then drive the bung in firmly with a mallet. The cider should age in this barrel a year or so.

In general people in colonial New England drank their beer and cider still, although sometimes their drinks were naturally carbonated by being sealed before fermentation was complete. In this modern day, effervescent beers and ciders are more compatible with other drinks we are used to. If you find still beer or cider unappetizing, you can easily give it a bit of fizz. Instead of ageing in a barrel, siphon the cider into bottles, adding one teaspoon of sugar per quart. Further fermentation will provide a light natural carbonation to the finished cider. Use crimp type caps or wire down the corks to withstand the added pressure. Let this cider ripen in the bottles for some months while the fermentation takes place.

This ageing in bottles often goes by the German name of "lager" fermentation and it may produce one problem for the modern drinker who is accustomed to clear drinks, since this further fermentation will produce lees in the bottom of the bottle. When the pressure is released, these lees will be stirred up and the cider will appear muddy. This does not affect the taste, but if for cosmetic reasons you want the cider to stay clear, there is a fairly simple way of proceeding. Store the sealed bottles upside down during the lager fermentation (a few months). After the sediment has settled in the neck, put the upside down bottles in the freezer. When the cider is solid, remove the frozen lees which will be in the neck and reseal while still frozen. If you use plastic champagne stoppers, which are hollow, all the sediment will come out with the stopper when removed.

One word of caution: do not try this technique with beer. Cider freezes into "slip ice," which is fairly soft and does not exert great pressure on the bottle. Beer, which behaves like water, freezes into a solid cake with a large coefficient of expansion, which will almost certainly shatter the bottle.

# Royal Cider

Although hard cider is alcoholic, the 5 percent content that results from fermenting the sweet cider made only from New England apples does not guarantee that the cider will keep well, particularly in hot weather. When the farmer could afford the time and money to do so, he would spike the cider with a distilled liquor. If he used apple brandy, the result was a very highly regarded drink known as Royal Cider or Cider Royal. This combination was often fortified up to the alcoholic concentration of a table wine.

Under this same name was another drink that was even stronger. Apple wine was fortified with apple brandy to give a drink much like sherry. In fact it was at times "sherryized" (which means that the barrels containing the wine and brandy mixture were left out

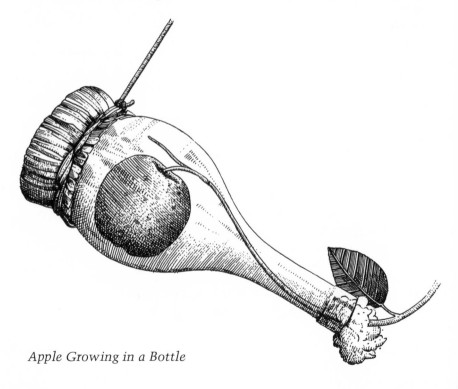

*Apple Growing in a Bottle*

in the hot sun to blend.) Apple brandy is a fairly harsh liquor and Royal Cider was sometimes mellowed by ageing the beverage after sherryizing. The mixture was sealed in a bottle in which an apple had been grown, not only to improve the taste but to delight the eye as well. A full-sized apple inside a bottle is quite a sight the first time it is seen. The farmers used to amaze strangers with tall tales of special shrink-drying techniques or their skill at "milking" whole apples through the necks of bottles.

# You Too Can Do It

A convenient way to try out this drink is to take four quarts of apple wine and add a "fifth" of apple brandy (often sold in liquor stores under the erroneous name of applejack.) This makes five quarts of Royal Cider. It can be kept hot all summer by storing the bottles in a hot attic. Use champagne bottles and either close them with crimp caps or wire down the corks, because when they get hot, the pressure builds up quite high in the bottles.

To try the apple-ageing technique, you must have available a bearing apple tree. Select a perfect fruit early enough in the spring so that the small apple will pass through the neck of whatever bottle you plan to use. A demijohn or fiasco is very convenient, since the wickerwork makes it easy to tie to. You can use a decanter, although it is a little hard to get the apple out if you want to use the decanter for something else later. Strip off all the side twigs and leaves from the branch holding the apple and slip the fruit into the center of the bottle. Tie the bottle to a convenient branch with the neck sloping downwards for rain drainage. Plug the entrance of the bottle with cotton to keep out the bugs and worms and leave it to grow for the whole summer. In the fall when the fruit is ripe, it is easy to pull the stem off the apple. Rinse the bottle and apple to clean it of bark and other debris and fill it up with sherryized Royal Cider. If you keep the apple covered with liquid it will last for years. To be effective as an ageing agent the apple should be in contact with the liquor for not less than six months.

# Apple Wine

Hard cider was the main thirst-quencher for the early settlers, but when sugar in some form was available, it was not uncommon to make a more alcoholic wine by continuing the fermentation beyond the hard cider stage. This was a process separate from the cider making. After the cider was fermented to completion, it was racked off into another barrel to separate it from the lees, raisins and sugar were added, and it was fermented a second time to raise the alcoholic content from the 5 percent cider to about 12 percent of apple wine. Maple syrup was often used as the sugar, since the timing of the processes was just about right. Fresh cider which started to ferment in October had gone as far as it could go, if kept in the warmth of the house, by March, when the sap began to run. The farmer therefore did not have to store the syrup but could add it directly to the cider barrel. Other common sugars that were used were honey, in which case the wine was called "cyser," or imported cane sugars, usually of the crude variety we now call "brown."

In restarting the second fermentation, added yeast was sometimes necessary but usually not. The farmers made their raisins by air-drying bunches of grapes hung from the house rafters so that the wild yeasts that were on the grapes were available to go to work as soon as the raisins were added to the cider.

# Modern Making

Fill a 10-gallon barrel right up to the top with sweet cider and close with a water seal. You can ferment this to hard cider with or without yeast. If you add yeast it will take two or three weeks; without added yeast it will take a month or more. When fermentation is complete, rack off the liquid to another barrel. Add to this second barrel four pounds of sugar or an equivalent amount of honey or maple syrup, and three pounds of raisins, and reseal with a fermentation lock. Fermentation should start up again and continue for a few months. If it does not, add more yeast. Let the barrel sit for a few weeks after the gas has stopped coming off, so that the lees will settle out, then rack the wine off into another barrel to age. This wine must be aged for at least a year before using.

A variation of this process which results in a mellower apple wine is to use brown sugar. If brown sugar is used, keep the wine under its water seal for a few months after the bubbling has stopped. Brown sugar tends to keep the second fermentation going, and you may have difficulty if you try to start the ageing too soon.

# Applejack

Applejack (or as it was also called, "cider oil") was one of the most common strong drinks made in the old New England countryside. Whereas the other strong drinks were made by distilling, either in small quantities and very slowly on the back of the kitchen stove or in larger quantities requiring a lot of work in gathering the wood and tending the fires, applejack came from hard cider by the process of fractional crystallization by freezing, which the weather took care of automatically.

The potency of the result is directly proportional to the coldness of the weather. The water freezes, forming ice that floats to the surface. The colder the temperature, the more ice is frozen out. Normal diurnal temperature fluctuations allow the liquid with higher alcoholic content to drain out of the crystal lattice of the ice during the day and refreeze during the night, gradually forming a greater and greater separation between the ice and the liquor.

When colored by dark-kerneled Indian corn, it was said to taste so much like Madeira wine that Europeans drank it without realizing the difference.

Real applejack cannot be made unless the temperature goes down below 0° Fahrenheit. However, a continuous variety of wines can be made depending on the severity of the winter. Measured alcohol percentages as a function of temperature are shown in graph 2, page 102. Applejack made in southern New England rarely exceeds about 25 percent alcohol, and in the north its alcoholic content can get much higher. The records show that the New

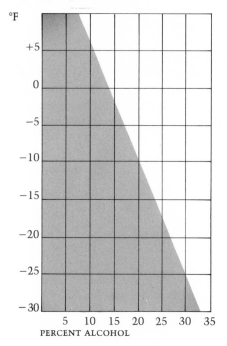

°F

PERCENT ALCOHOL

## The Colder the Weather, The More Potent

England weather has not changed in character since Colonial days, and the common tales one hears from the farmers of the tremendous potency of their grandfathers' applejack do not come from the proof-strength of the drink. Stories get taller in the telling, and some of the alleged effects of applejack are undoubtedly embroidery. On the other hand, fractional crystallization is a fairly common chemical technique for purifying crystals, which implies that the ice gets purer and purer as the process goes on and the impurities become concentrated in the remaining liquid. The after-effects of drinking can often be laid much more to "impurities" in strong drink than the actual alcoholic content, so that the reputation of applejack may be quite justified. The state of intoxication that followed unrestrained drinking of applejack was called "apple palsy."

# Modern Equivalent

If there is any place where one can buy real applejack I have not been able to find it. If you want to taste this most popular of old New England drinks you will have to make it. What is sold in New England shops as applejack and from Normandy as calvados is apple brandy, not real applejack. Brandy is made by distilling, not freezing, and is very different. Distilling purifies the alcohol and leaves the impurities behind, to be discarded, while freezing purifies the water (to be discarded) and leaves all the taste in the alcohol.

It was not because of this increase in taste that the farmer used freezing instead of distillation. Distillation over a fire took a lot of wood and the farmer had more important uses for his labor.

To make applejack, start with no less than five gallons of sweet cider and ferment it under a water seal to completion. This will take about a month. The hard cider than should be racked off into another container, which should be put outside to freeze. If the climate is sufficiently severe to assure an extended period of time when the nights will be below zero, the cider may be frozen in a barrel and tapped some time in mid-winter after the temperature has dipped to $-20°$F or lower. In northern New England you do not really have to see what is going on, but can let nature take its course unsupervised. However, if temperatures of zero or below occur only a few times in the winter, you have to attend to the separation with more care, and a transparent carboy should be used so that you can observe the rate of progress of the fractional crystallization.

When the nights have been cold enough (and the days not so warm as to melt everything) to freeze the top layer of the cider to thickness of an inch or more of very white ice, siphon off the liquid into another carboy, leaving the ice behind as waste. Keep fractionating the cider in this fashion all winter. As the volume of liquid gets less, it becomes convenient to move to gallon jugs and rather than use a siphon, the liquid can be poured off through and around the ice.

Good applejack will result if the concentration gets to a point where it will no longer freeze at zero or below. This will amount to a reduction in liquid volume of at least seven eighths of the amount you start with, and sometimes as much as nine tenths. The stronger the concentrate, obviously, the smaller the yield.

Applejack is a very dry drink and as far as we can tell colonial New Englanders drank it just as it came from the barrel. However, our modern taste treats applejack as a liqueur. These are customarily sweet and so it fits the modern palate better to sweeten the liquor as it is bottled. The bottling should be done while the applejack is still cold. Add one tablespoon full of activated charcoal (to help it age) and 4 tablespoons of sugar to each pint, cap and age for at least two years.

In southern New England it is by no means certain that the temperature will always be cold enough to make good applejack every year. However, even if the temperature only gets down to 5° or 10°F, the concentrate is still worth bottling and ageing as it makes a pleasant light apple wine. Of course it is perfectly practical to bottle what does not concentrate sufficiently one year and keep it to try the next. To do this, seal the concentrate in quart bottles; then about the following January, empty these bottles into gallon jugs and continue the freezing process.

# Pears

In many sections of New England during colonial days, pears were as common a fruit as apples and the farmers used them in much the same way. Particularly in southern New England, "perry" was as common as cider, and all the recipes from hard ciders and wines can be extended to perries.

Not all varieties of pears are as easy to handle as apples. Pears that are hard when ripe can be processed just as apples. However, the kinds of pears which are soft when ripe do not go through the cider press properly. They do not break when they are crushed but tend to turn into a mush that not only clogs up the crusher but squirts out of the sides of the pressing bucket when the pressure is applied. Because of this pears were often mixed with apples. This added an almost infinite variety of final product. Nevertheless, if pears were used at all in the pressing, the drink was always referred to as "perry" even when a large fraction of cider was present.

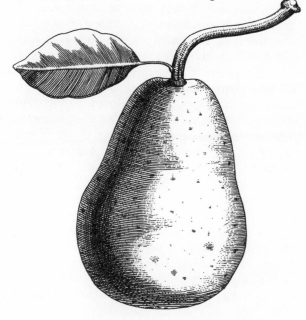

# CHAPTER FIVE

# Grapes

When the Vikings first landed on these shores, they were so im-
pressed by the profusion of grapes that they gave the name Vine-
land to their newly discovered land. Grapes are indigenous to all of
the area and were to be found in such quantities that the settlers
saw wine as a potential natural resource of great value. This led to
a most curious clash between the European educated taste for wine
and a continent where a different species of grape had developed.

One of the first agricultural products that each of the early settlements promoted was the manufacture of wine from the prolific
harvests so readily available throughout the forests and fields all
along the coast. It very soon became evident that the wine made
from these grapes had a very different taste, unacceptable to European markets. But surely a land where grapes grew wild in such
abundance would welcome imported strains that would please the
European palate. Colony after colony brought over their enologists
and agricultural experts to set out and cultivate the British, French
and Spanish grapes. It is a history of complete failure, yet the
amazing fact is that it took so long for one enthusiast after another
to finally become convinced that the European species *Vitis vinifera* could not thrive where the American *Vitis labrusca* grew in
profusion. It was over 200 years of frustration. Lord Delaware
wrote to the London Company in 1616;

*In every boske and hedge, and not farr from our pallisade gates we
have thousands of goodly vines running along and leaving to every
tree, which yealds a plentiful grape in their kinde. Let me ap-
pealed, then, to knowledge if these naturall vines were planted,
dressed and ordered by skillfull venearoons, whether we might
not make a perfect grape and fruitfull vintage in short time?*

In the early nineteenth century American agricultural experts finally turned their attention to hybrid varieties of the *labrusca* grape which would yield a taste acceptable to the wine-drinking public.

These attempts to introduce the European wine grape into the eastern part of this continent were not small operations but major attempts to promote a great industry. Growing from fairly small beginnings in New England when John Winthrop, the Governor of Massachusetts Bay Colony, took over "Governor's Island" in Boston Harbor in 1629 for this purpose, and the extensive plantations at the mouth of the Piscataqua River in Maine, thousands of acres of land and hundreds of thousands of imported vines were dedicated to this great attempt, all doomed to failure after a few decades. And all this time, nothing was being done with the native

American grape. It was an outcast which, when finally noticed by the professionals, almost wiped out the European wine industry.

Native to eastern United States is a small aphid-like insect called a phylloxera. Labrusca grape vines developed through the ages an immunity to this aphid (which causes the galls on our hickory, oak, and willow trees) but when European viniculturalists imported some American grapes to Europe for experiments around 1860, disaster struck. The insect devasted the French vineyards, nearly destroying the wine industry there, and quickly spread to other European countries. Its fatal effect occurs when the lice attacks the roots, and no effective remedy was discovered to save the roots of the *vinifera* vines. Nowadays all European grapevines in phylloxera-infested areas are grafted onto native American root stock.

As if it were not enough that the phylloxera totally destroys the Old World grape vines in a few years, there are three other pests to which the *vinifera* grape is susceptible in the New World but to which native grapes are relatively immune: the black-rot, the downy mildew, and the powdery mildew. The European grape has no chance east of the Rocky Mountains.

The *labrusca* itself seems to have been completely ignored in the early American era. The various types were not named, and the vines were not cultivated by the early farmers. Just as the settlers did not plant blackberries, raspberries, blueberries, and currants, but went berrying in the woods and fields to collect their crop, so with grapes. The woods were full of them and it was easy to pick a few hundred pounds for their year's supply of wine.

While the educated Europeans coming to America rejected the wild grapes and spent generations in the hopeless effort to change the American scene, those who were willing to absorb the new life, including new tastes, developed a type of wine that became as characteristically American as apple pie and cider. The native grape imparts to the wine an odor and taste called "foxiness" and for this reason was often called a "Fox-grape." It has a sort of muskiness or spicy fruity taste which when found in European wines denoted an inferior wine. Nevertheless the early Americans grew to prefer the taste, and in fact considered European wine lacking in character because it was not foxy.

After the term was firmly attached to the labrusca grape, early writers about the American scene speculated widely on where the term came from. Thus Beauchamp Plantagenet (in his *New Albion,* 1648) thought the term came from the old word "to intoxicate," which was "to fox." Several writers reported that the odor of the grapes suggested that of a fox, others that the dense pubescence or wool on the underside of the leaf was a foxy color, and another thought that it was by this odor that skunks, foxes, and raccoons were attracted to the vines. No one really knew.

The grape itself is small and blue or black-skinned, though green below the skin. It is well adapted to a cold climate since it has a thick "slip" skin. The skin is not firmly attached to the pulp. This skin provides good insulation for the fruit beneath. Because so many of the settlers tried to establish vinifera grape vineyards, by the accidents of wind, insects, or deliberate hybridization, the pollens from many struggling viniferas found their way to the native labruscas and there developed a wide variety of native New England grapes, all hybrids of the labrusca.

## Your Challenge

It is not an easy task to reproduce the native grape wine of the New England settlers. The primeval forest abounded in grapes, but fire, lumbering, farmers, and sheep ranching have destroyed the primeval forest. Virtually none is left in New England. Though the fox-grape is still to be found throughout, our second-growth forests are by no means so luxuriant in grapes, and collecting eighty pounds of the wild berries to ferment to ten gallons of wine is usually impractical. The surest way is to grow your own, but this is not as easy as it might seem because for the past 150 years viniculturalists have been bending all their efforts to hybridize out of the labrusca the very foxiness that characterized early colonial grape wine. Everything that you read and hear will tell you that the grapes you want "do not make acceptable wines." Our cultural bias still demands that wine must taste like vinifera, and the further toward labrusca it tastes, the "worse" it is. Your challenge, therefore, is to throw off your Old World heritage and become truly New World American.

Fortunately the foxiness of wild grapes is a strong taste, so a relatively few pounds of grapes from the wild will put you well on the way toward the right colonial taste. The best way to accomplish this in the long run is to locate some well-bearing wild vines and transfer them to your vineyard. Old grapevine roots grow deep and long, and it is useless to try to dig them up. Rather, you should use the process of "layering." Dig a short trench in the spring next to a vigorous vine, lay in one of its long woody stems or canes and cover with two to five inches of earth. When shoots come up from this buried cane, cut off its connection to the main vine. These individual shoots will be the root stock to be transplanted to the vineyard the following spring. Grow some of these wild grapes to maturity (this will take about five years) so that you will have some of their taste in your finished wine, but they will not bear profusely and you will want either to buy some of the modern hybrids or graft some of these hybrids onto most of your root stock to get your yield up to some reasonable amount. It takes fifteen to twenty vines to produce ten gallons of wine a year considering the variations of the weather and the depredations of rodents, birds, wasps, and small boys.

The root-stock vines will be ready for grafting when the main cane is one quarter to three eighths of an inch thick. Then remove the earth from around the vine to a depth of two inches. Cut off the stock squarely at the height of the surface of the ground and cleft graft (see above page oo) onto it a single scion of the same diameter cut to two buds. Tie up the graft with yarn. Do not use grafting wax but mound up the earth around the graft. Keep track of the grafted area during the summer, cutting off all the roots that start growing from the scion and all the shoots that come from the root stock.

Your scions can come from a nursery, a friendly vineyardist, or your own vines. Wherever they come from, arrange to have several kinds of grapes so that you can adjust your crop to suit your taste. You can, of course, layer-propagate from your own vines. The layered vines come true to their parents, so that there is no need to graft if you want to keep the same type of grape. Remember, however, that this is a very leisurely procedure, since, as you plan to change the percentage of your crop to different types of grapes, it takes about five years to establish a well-bearing grapevine. Once you have your vineyard balanced to your taste, however, your product will be uniform year after year.

In choosing cultivated hybrids, be guided by the general principle that the older the hybrid the more labrusca the taste. The most popular of the early labrusca hybrids was the accidentally produced Catawba. It is a dull, purplish-red grape with a rather thick skin which so captured the American fancy in the early nineteenth century that Henry Wadsworth Longfellow sung its praises:

> But Catawba wine has a taste more divine,
> More dulcet, delicious and dreamy.
> There grows no vine, by the haunted Rhine,
> By the Danube or Guadalquiver,
> Nor island or cape, that bears such a grape
> As grows by the beautiful River.

Another of the accidental hybrids that was early recognized and named was the Clinton. This is a black grape that was found in 1819 and was given its name by Hugh White (later a member of Congress), who was a freshman at Hamilton College in Clinton, New York, at the time. Another black grape which some experts claim is not a hybrid at all but a pure labrusca is the Isabella. It was widely cultivated before 1800 but was not named until 1816, by George Gibbs, a merchant in Brooklyn, New York, in honor of his wife.

The most famous of all American grapes is the Concord. It is a black grape covered with a blue bloom with a thick skin and pale green flesh. It was discovered at a time when there was great interest in searching for new American grape varieties by planting vast numbers of wild grape seeds to see what would result. The type of grape which grows from seed bears little relation to the parent vine and this game of chance intrigued hundreds of amateurs and professionals alike. One such enthusiast was Ephraim W. Bull of Concord, Massachusetts, who spent most of his 90 years growing grape seedlings. In the fall of 1843 he planted a wild seed that bore its first fruit in 1849. It had been planted next to a fence in which Catawbas were growing and it has been widely assumed that cross-pollination occurred which resulted in what Horace Greeley called "the grape for the millions." In the New England area it is easy to grow. It is prolific in its fruiting and subject to few diseases, and it ripens easily during the short growing season.

An offspring of the Concord is the Worden. It was grown from a seed of a Concord by Schuyler Worden of Minetto, New York, who was playing the grape game in 1863. Its advantage over the Concord is that it ripens two weeks earlier. It is so similar in appearance that they are often confused, although the pulp of the Worden is softer and the berries are juicier. It is considered by the experts to be a true labrusca.

The leading American green grape is the Niagara, a labrusca-vinifera hybrid. One of the parents of the Niagara is the Concord and, as with it, the foxiness of the wild labrusca is retained. It was fruited for the first time in 1872 in Lockport, Niagara County, New York, and accepted as a variety in 1885. In spite of its late arrival, it is the only one of the modern commercially available white grapes that retains the real characteristics of the old New England fox-grapes.

The main problem with growing grapes for wine in New England is to provide the vines with enough sunshine to assure that the berries ripen before the autumn is too far advanced. The few early farmers who did plant vineyards spread their vines far apart, often over old dead trees, so that the vines did not shade each other, or they planted against a south-facing stone wall to take advantage of the heat retention property of such a system. If one has lots of space, these techniques are still good to copy, but if space is limited, the vines really do tend to get in each other's way and to slow down the ripening process, and the berries do have to be vine ripened to be successful for wine.

The more direct sunlight that falls on the leaves, the greater is the energy available for the necessary photosynthesis. Modern experts have studied the geometry of vineyard architecture in great detail. Their studies show that in clear weather 40 percent of the absorbed light comes from diffused sky light on the top of the vine, about 50 percent is direct sunlight absorbed by the vine sides, and the rest by sky light absorbed on the vine sides. If 60 percent of the energy is absorbed by the vine sides, the geographic orientation of the vines is important. The fact is that during New England summers, four times as much sunlight falls on the vine sides when the trellises run north and south than if they were oriented east and west. Of less importance is the height of vine sides, though studies have shown that north-south vines nine feet tall intercept 50 percent more sunlight at this latitude than if the vine curtain is three feet high. A further refinement in trellis design to increase the sun exposure is a "double curtain" trellis, where vines that are planted in a row are trained on a double trellis. The vertical supporting posts terminate in a four-foot horizontal member. The wires or poles that support the vines are attached to the end of these T-shaped pieces and the vines, spaced six to eight feet apart, are trained to alternate sides to create a "double curtain" to increase the sun exposure. This gains the plants another 25 percent of sunlight, all of which gets more and more important the further north one goes.

Before we get off the subject of grapevines, we should say a bit about pruning. You will not have healthy vines and a good crop unless you prune drastically every winter. After the vines are well frozen you can prune anytime until the sap starts to run in the spring. Except when you are trying to shape the vines, every new cane should be pruned back to not more than six buds, and all canes that grow on the main vertical trunk should be eliminated completely.

Commercial growers use various sophisticated instruments to determine when the sugar content is just right for picking, but the old-fashioned way of waiting until the birds begin to attack the berries gives excellent results. If you use this method, you have to keep watching for the birds to move in, and when they do, the

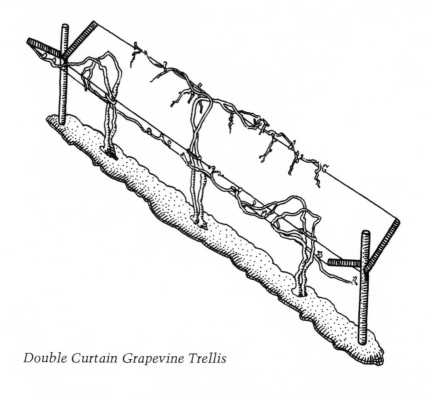

*Double Curtain Grapevine Trellis*

sooner you get to the vines and strip all the fruit, the greater will be the yield. Bird-damaged berries do not keep well, so you have to beat the birds to the main crop. Because different varieties ripen at different times, if you have various different kinds of grapes in your vineyard be careful to pick only the particular type which the birds have told you have come to full ripeness.

## Grape Wine

There was considerable difference between the grape wine that the early farmers made to quench their thirst along with their beer and cider and the native wines that they looked on as a healthful supplement to their meals. The difference centered around the availability of sugar. The New England weather does not produce a grape high in sugar. Even when ripe, the wine made from grapes alone is very dry, so dry in fact that the alcoholic content is more like beer than the normal 10–20 percent common in all wines of today. This very dry wine was, however, a common thirst quencher. On the other hand when honey, maple, or corn syrup or sugar was available, the settlers made a table wine similar in strength to what is made today.

Nowhere is the contrast greater between the taste of old colonial beverages and their modern equivalent than in grape wines. Be prepared, therefore, for some new taste sensations when you open your first bottle of old farmer's wine. You have several choices, all of which will recreate some colonial's familiar wine. If you crush, press, and ferment the grapes just as they come from the vines, you will produce an extremely fruity bouquet and a reasonable strength. This type of wine takes a lot of grapes—10 pounds per gallon—and may be unpleasantly dry for modern taste. On the other hand it has such a good bouquet that if you make it for your own education you will find it very useful for the main ingredient in hot mulled wine (see below, page 000). A considerably more efficient way of using the grapes is to soak the crushed berries in water to draw out more of the sugar and taste. The osmotic pressure is such that this drawing process works very well and the resulting must is not found to be inferior in either taste or strength to the straight grape juice provided that not more than one gallon of water per fifteen pounds of grapes is used. Old instructions often warn against this method as producing an unhealthful wine, and from our modern perspective we can guess that this was probably because of the danger of contaminated water. However, if one uses pure water, this is a recommended procedure. Adding sugar produced a wine similar to our usual modern table wine. Straining the must of all skins led to a white wine, and leaving the skins in the fermenting juice (unless only Niagara grapes were used) gave a rosé or red wine.

# Modern Equivalent

It is just as important in recreating colonial wines to enjoy the product of your labor as it is to use old New England grapes. So at least start with a table wine. If you want to attempt the stranger-tasting wines later it is easy to modify the following method by leaving out the sugar or the water.

Ten gallons of wine is a good amount to deal with. Mash up sixty pounds of grapes picked off their stems. In the old days this was usually done in a "stone" jar with a wooden potato masher. A plastic tub or garbage pail, though not as romantic, works just as well. Grape crushers (like the crusher on a cider press though with much less clearance) are available and if you make very much wine, they save a great deal of labor. The idea is not to break the seeds, which would put a bitter taste into the wine. This grape-crushing process is accomplished in European wine-making areas by trampling on the fruit by foot. I can find no records that this was a New England technique, but for some reason this part of the process has so captured popular imagination that almost the only question that will be asked when it is learned that you make your wine from your own grapes will be, "Do you walk on your grapes with your bare feet?"

Pour ten gallons of boiling water over the mash and let it stand for three days covered as tightly as possible to discourage the fruit flies. After three days strain the liquid into a barrel. You will get a lot more juice if you can squeeze the remaining pulp. The early farmer who lacked a press would wring out the must from the crushed grapes by twisting them in rough cloth or burlap bags. This works, though it is a lot of labor, which is avoided if you have a wine press. It was much more common for an early farmer to have a cider than a wine press. The slots in the basket of a cider press are too wide to be useful for grapes, but if the basket is lined with crushed apples to keep the grape pulp from being squeezed out sideways it works very well. This does not materially effect the taste of the grape wine, and it is a good technique to follow.

Add thirty cups (fifteen pounds) of honey or sugar. If you are using your own grapes, you may not need any yeast, since the skins will be covered with wild yeast, but if the grapes have been commercially washed, you will probably have to add yeast. Modern wine yeasts are carefully cultivated not only for their distinctive tastes but also to maximize their flocculation properties to enhance the clarity of the finished wine. This is a quality that sophisticated wine experts strive to achieve. Cultivated yeasts have to be very carefully protected so that they do not become contaminated with wild yeasts that do not have this property. Wines fermented by natural yeasts were almost always cloudy unless they were artificially "fined" with a variety of techniques that included isinglass, egg albumen, or filtering. Since the "bloom" on grape skins consists of a waxy film that collects yeasts, there is always a lot of wild yeast on the grape skins. The old farmers did not care a whit for clarity and drank their cloudy wine for its taste.

For the seasonal wines and cider the farmer usually relied on the wild yeasts available in the musts to get the fermentation started. However, the yeasts in the lees of old wines could be rejuvenated by careful cultivation in a fruit juice and sugar "starter" solution. The recipes for doing this were often published. This is impossible with many wines of today because they are often pasteurized, but in the old days this method of guaranteeing good keeping quality was unknown and the lees from old wines were kept and reused. To prepare a starter, about half a pint of must was boiled with a tablespoon of sugar and a teaspoon of lemon juice. When cooled, it was poured into a clean bottle and the lees from an old wine was added. The bottle was plugged with a small piece of cloth and put in a warm place for a few days. It was shaken occasionally to promote aeration and was used when active fermentation was obvious.

Red wine is made by fermenting the colored skins of blue or black grapes with the must. Ten or twenty pounds of Concord or Worden grapes mashed but not squeezed can be added to the fermenting liquid to give a richly colored red wine.

Add the liquid from the pressing to the barrel into which you poured the strained juice and stop the cask with a water seal. If you are relying on natural yeasts, watch the water seal carefully to make sure that fermentation gets started. If there is no sign of $CO_2$ emission in a week, open up the barrel and add some yeast.

Allow the wine to ferment to completion. This takes three to five months. When activity has stopped, rack off into another barrel, drive a bung in tightly, and let the wine age a minimum of one year, then siphon it off into bottles.

# CHAPTER SIX

# Family Wines

The greatest volume of beverages consumed by the farmers by far was beer, cider, and grape wine to quench their thirst. But there was another whole area of wine-making which served a very different purpose. In today's society when the minster or neighbors come to call or the family gathers for christenings or funerals, tea or coffee and cakes usually appear as a focus for gathering to talk and visit. Not so in early farm communities, where sweet wines, cordials, or punches were likely to be served. These were so much a matter of individual making that recipes of the day emphasized the poisonous and ill-tasting ingredients to be avoided rather than what to use.

Such flowers as lilies of the valley, privet, and laurel were reported as poisonous. The most common warning was against lilac blossoms. The lilac was not native to New England but was brought from England very early, and almost every New England farm house had a profusion of these sweet-smelling flowers in the spring. We now know that lilac blossoms contain a high concentration of digitalis, a powerful cardiac stimulant and diuretic, and the warning against their use was well-founded.

It is also clear from travelers' accounts and old diaries that particular families were immensely proud of their products and vied with each other for excellence and novelty. Even a casual look through old records will give such a long list of basic ingredients that you soon get the idea that almost anything in the kitchen garden or back fields and woods became a prime target for a family wine, often called "folk" wines. Even without an exhaustive library of books on old wine-making, one can find published recipes for wines made from apple, apricot, balm, carrot, celery, cherry, chokecherry, clove, clover, coconut, corn stalk, cowslip, cranberry, cyprus, dandelion, date, elderberry, elder flower, ginger, goldenrod,

gooseberry, grape, grape leaf, grape tendril, hawthorn, hop, Jerusalem artichoke, juniper, lemon, lettuce, loganberry, marigold, may
blossom, mint, mulberry, nettle, oak leaf, orange, pansy, parsnip,
peach, peapod, pineapple, plum, potato, potato stalk, primrose,
pumpkin, quince, raisin, raspberry, rhubarb, rice, rose, rose hip,
rowenberry (mountain ash), sage, spinach, spruce, squash, strawberry, sycamore, tomato, turnip, walnut, wheat, whortleberry,
yarrow.

# Try a Few

One does not need a different recipe for each kind of family wine
that can be made from whatever is growing around you, so we will
divide the possibilities into flowers, roots, leaves, and berries, and
take typical examples from each.

Although flowers contain the proper enzymes for wine production, they do not have much nectar, so that fairly large amounts of
sugar or honey need to be added to ferment them. The most common of all colonial flower wines was made from dandelion blossoms. The dandelion was not a native plant but was brought from
England by the very early settlers as a garden flower. It was particularly popular for wine making because the flowers are rich in
yeasts, and fermentation is therefore easy and reliable. In fact dandelion blossoms were often used as yeast starters in the spring,
since the other two sources of wild yeasts, the apple and the grape,
were autumn fruits and their yeasts were not kept over the winter.

Most of the flower and vegetable wines have delicate tastes, but
dandelion wine has a distinctive and robust flavor. For this reason
one often finds reference to its use in cooking, particularly whole
birds and small animals, like rabbits and squirrels, and frogs' legs.
The colonial Americans ate a great many songbirds. Although the
slaughter of these small birds was eventually made illegal, the
early farmer found trapping or liming songbirds a ready source of
food without the use of ammunition, and a lot of dandelion wine
was used in their cooking.

The trick about making good dandelion wine is not to let the

*Dandelions*

tiniest piece of stalk get into the wine-making process. Pull off the petals by holding the yellow petals with the fingers of one hand while holding the green base of the flower head with the other and then pulling the head apart. If you do not take this trouble you will get an unpleasant resinous taste in the finished wine.

Gather a gallon of heads. After removing the petals, put them in a glass jar or jug with a tightfitting lid and add three quarts of boiling water. Let this stand for seven days, stirring at least once a day. At the end of this time, strain out the petals. Boil one and one half pounds of sugar or honey in a pint of water, cool, and add to the liquor one cake of yeast and the juice of two lemons. Seal with a water lock and let it ferment for seven days. Then pour carefully into a clean jar, leaving as much of the deposit behind as you can. Boil another one and one half pounds of sugar or honey in another pint of water, cool, and add to the liquor. Ferment to completion. This double fermentation prevents the wine from becoming too sweet. When the fermentation has ceased, bottle and seal the liquor and let it age at least 6 months to a year before drinking. It has the characteristics of an after-dinner wine. It is strong (17 percent), sweet, and aromatic.

Wine can be made of red clover blossoms in just the same way. Use the same petal-stripping method of separating the sweet petals from the green part of the head. With the petals removed from most of the common edible flowers, like day lily, fuchsia, gladiolus, marigold, nasturtium, pansy, primrose, rose, or violet, in the direct "love-me, love-me-not" technique, they all make good wines by the recipe just given. Complex flowers like lavender and goldenrod require more care in pulling off the blossom clusters without getting the leaves mixed with the blossoms, but they are also good for wine making, and it is worth the trouble.

Berry wines were also very popular. Blackberry, cranberry, chokecherry, currant, elderberry, gooseberry, loganberry, raspberry, and strawberry were all used, depending on what were readily available, and the wines were all made by the same recipe. For each gallon of wine, four quarts of berries were crushed with a wooden spoon or pestle. Nowadays it is much simpler ʻ·ɔ run the berries through an electric food blender. Pour one quart of boiling water over the mashed berries, stir, and let them cool for a few hours. Then boil one pound of sugar for a minute or so in three pints of water, allow it to cool, mix it with the fruit pulp, and add one half cup of lemon juice and a tablespoon of yeast. Ferment for seven days. Strain out the pulp, boil another pound of sugar in one pint of water, cool, and add to the strained must. Ferment again for another ten days. Then boil a third pound of sugar in a pint of water, add again when cooled, and ferment to completion. Bottle and age for at least six months.

A surprising number of vegetables were used in making family wines, and reports can be found of the use of beets, carrots, celery, Jerusalem artichokes, onions, parsnips, peapods, potatoes, and turnips. They were all made about the same way. The vegetables were peeled and then boiled until tender. The amounts used were four pounds of vegetables per gallon of water. These wines were bland, and cloves or ginger roots were often added in the boiling to give the wine more character. You should try some of these yourself.

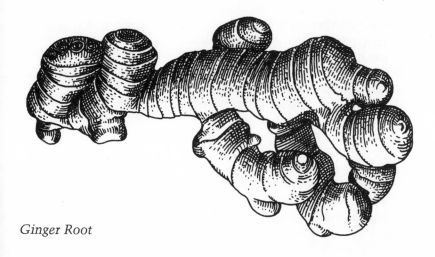

*Ginger Root*

Using your own imagination on herbs or spices will be quite in accord with the way it was done long ago. One ingredient often used was tea.

Strain out the vegetable pulp. Add three pounds of sugar, one half cup of lemon juice, and a tablespoon of yeast. Ferment to completion under a water seal. Vegetable wines take longer to mature, so after boiling let them age for two years before drinking.

Two very popular wines made from common garden products were rhubarb and parsley. For rhubarb, use three pounds of rhubarb to three pounds of sugar per gallon of finished wine. Slice the rhubarb thinly, cover with dry sugar, and wait until the sugar has gone to juice. Strain off the juice and wash out the sugar that has remained entrapped in the pulp by stirring in water and straining again. Add yeast and ferment.

According to herbal lore, there was nothing like parsley to keep rheumatism or arthritis under control, and no way of taking it was quite as pleasant as a daily glassful of parsley wine. Simmer six cups of parsley with the rind of two lemons in three quarts of water for half an hour. Strain into a jar, dissolve two pounds of sugar in it, add the juice of the lemons and yeast and let it ferment for two weeks. Then rack it off into another jug and let the fermentation go to completion. This wine needs not be aged more than six months before it is ready to drink.

Another popular family wine which matures quickly was made from rose hips. Three quarts of ripe rose hips can be crushed with a mallet or put through a food chopper or meat grinder. Put the mash into a crock and pour a gallon of boiling water over it. Keep the crock in a warm place for a week, stirring and squeezing the mash with your hands at least once a day. Then strain, add lemon juice and yeast, and ferment to completion.

Finally there was a whole class of wines made from leaves. Here is a typical recipe—for oak leaf wine, which I found particularly good. Pick 4 quarts of very young oak leaves in the early spring when, according to one old set of instructions, "the leaves are the size of a mouse's ear." Pour four pints of boiling water over the leaves, let stand for a day, and then strain. Warm the liquid to dissolve two pounds of sugar. Add one half cup lemon juice and, when cool, one tablespoon of yeast. Add water to make a volume of one gallon, and ferment.

Tree leaves should only be used in the early spring, but potato or grape leaves (and tendrils) can be used until early summer. Leaf vegetables such as spinach or lettuce can be used all summer.

# Ageing

Wines improve and mellow with age as a result of the many complex chemical reactions that continue to take place after fermentation has ceased. Concurrent and consecutive oxidation, reduction, and esterification mature the wine. Ethyl alcohol is oxidized to acetaldehyde and acetic acid, while a portion of the higher alcohols are converted to their respective aldehydes and acids. Acetaldehyde and other aldehydes combine with the alcohols to form acetals, and since both aldehydes and acetals are fragrant, they add to the bouquet of the wines. Also combinations between the various acids and alcohols form esters whose fruity aroma appears in the bouquet.

A maturing wine needs a supply of air to allow these oxidation reactions to proceed, but too much impairs the wine by overoxidation, mostly through the formation of too much acetaldehyde. An important factor that affects the rate of maturing is volume. Small quantities of wine mature faster than large volumes under identical conditions, but the best quality is achieved when wines are matured fairly slowly.

Bulk storage in wood brings out the best in a wine because the finely porous nature of wood allows the slow but continuous entry of air, from which dust and bacteria have been filtered, and usually in quantities small enough to cause no problem of overoxidation. To get the right amount of oxygen requires, however, the right size barrel. As barrel size changes, so does the ratio of their surface area to their volume. If this ratio is too large, the wine will get too much oxygen, and if too small, not enough. Thousands of years ago it was discovered that wooden containers were porous enough to

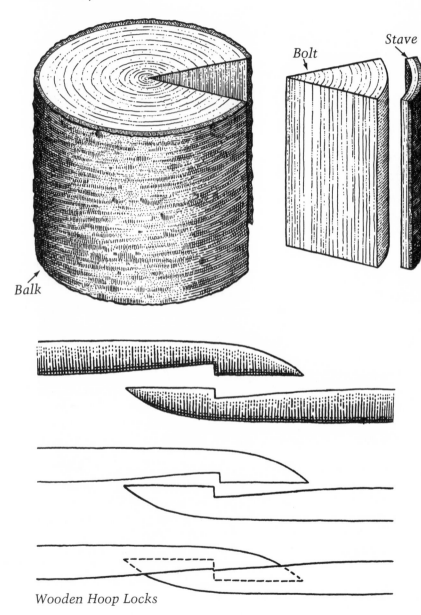

Balk

Bolt

Stave

Wooden Hoop Locks

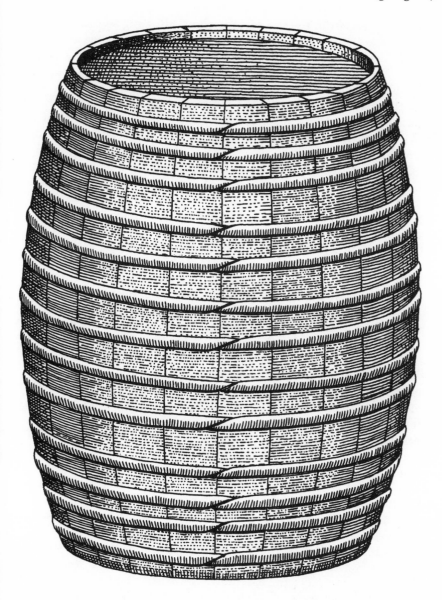

allow this oxidation to take place without allowing so much air to be in contact with the liquid as to spoil it. Not all woods are suitable, of course, since some are too porous and some are too impervious. White oak, a common New England wood, has all of the desirable characteristics as well as having a pleasant, slightly vanilla-like flavor. In addition, the white oak wood provides tannin, which helps to clarify the wine, and other extractives which add pleasant taste traces that enhance the overall excellence of the beverages.

All the important features of a barrel are dictated by the characteristics of the wood and the way that it grows. Without going into the constructional details of a barrel, a very sophisticated technology requiring special jigs and other tools, it may be of interest to see how much of this technology is governed by the raw materials, even though it is peripheral to actual wine-making.

First the shape. Although barrel staves have been made by machines of one sort or another for many generations, their original form was dictated by the way wood could be split with an axe, wedge, or chisel. The simple sketch will illustrate the point. A length of tree trunk was sawed into a section called by the cooper a "balk." This was first split into quarters and then into sections called "bolts." A bolt was then split into "staves" parallel to the grain, which was, of course, cylindrical in form, and thus the basic shape of the barrel was determined.

To make the lateral compression between staves necessary to keep water in or out, the staves were shaved toward the ends with a drawknife so that the center of the stave was wider than its ends; for example, for a ten-gallon barrel the staves are about twenty-two inches long and the ends of the staves are about one half inch narrower than the center. The staves were then grooved at the ends to hold a circular barrel head made of five or six boards gasketed with "flagging" made of cat-tail reeds, all the pieces being held together in a jig, and a hoop was forced onto the end. The whole affair was inverted over a box of glowing coals to heat the staves, so that they would be pliable. Hoops of differing sizes were then driven on to complete the assembly. An expert cooper would have shaped all the staves so that they would fit snugly together in the final assembly. Where iron was available, hoops were made of sheet or scrap iron, riveted together. For the pioneer farmer, however, iron was scarce and during the early years hoops were made of hickory or ash wood. The rings were ingeniously connected together by two interlocking hooks shaped like the barbs on fish-hooks or harpoons. These hooks were whittled on both ends of the wooden hoop and fitted snugly together, as shown in the figure. Naturally the wooden hoops were not as strong as those of iron, so that many more wooden hoops were used to hold the barrels together than when they were made of iron.

No barrel is water-tight when the wood is dry, but the wood of a good barrel soaked for a week or so will force all the staves and barrel-head boards together to provide an excellent liquid container.

As we have said, the size of a barrel controls to a large extent the satisfactory ageing of wines and ciders. It is a characteristic of the geometry of any hollow container that the ratio between the surface area of the container and its volume becomes greater as the volume becomes smaller. Thus the surface-to-volume ratio of a small barrel with its relatively larger surface area per gallon volume gives a greater exposure to the air than that of a larger cask. If the barrel is small, the wine or cider therefore ages more rapidly. If it is too small, too much air is available and the wine may spoil before the beneficial extracts in the wood have been leached out. If the barrel is big, the surface-to-volume ratio is small and it can be that not enough oxygen gets to the liquid to age it properly. (The barrel must always be full. See below.) It is interesting that the size of a white oak barrel maneuverable by one man is just about right for the home-ageing of wines and ciders. This is shown in graph 3, page 130, which is for barrels of round cross-sections. (Oval shaped barrels have 15 to 20 percent greater surface-to-volume ratios.) It is hard to believe that this was not one of the main reasons why white oak was preferred.

Commercial wineries, inns, and taverns stored their wines in much larger units, but if they were ageing them in large barrels, they frequently racked them off into other barrels to improve their quality. Any racking or drawing off into other barrels aerated the

## *Barrel size*

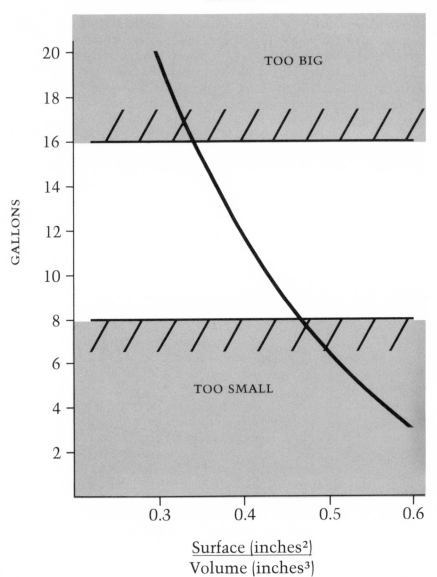

TOO BIG

GALLONS

TOO SMALL

20
18
16
14
12
10
8
6
4
2

0.3  0.4  0.5  0.6

Surface (inches²)
Volume (inches³)

liquor in the process and introduced sufficient oxygen to provide the oxidation of ageing. Here again it is interesting to note that a barrel difficult for a single man to lift was left alone and the liquid was moved. (A 16-gallon barrel full of wine weighs about 150 pounds.)

One very important fact in ageing wine, beers, and ciders in barrels, which has been known for a long time, is that the barrel needs to be full to overflowing before the bung is pounded in. Any air space over the wine is dangerous to the health of the wine. When liquors were being made in large quantities, this posed no problem, since there was always more liquid available to fill up the barrel. The individual farmer, however, was often faced with the problem of a half-full barrel after his entire product had been barreled. He would collect solid glass balls or china eggs to drop into the barrels to eliminate the ullage. One also finds old instructions suggesting the use of smooth stones and pebbles. Since rocks are slightly soluble in wine, this led to a cloudy product but did not affect the taste particularly. Since the early settlers drank from wood, leather, china, or pewter, the lack of clarity made little noticeable difference.

# Modern Equivalents

White oak barrels are available on the commercial market, so buying one for ageing wines and ciders is not a big problem. However, barrels are sometimes paraffined on the inside to seal against leakage. This destroys their usefulness for ageing and should be avoided.

Good barrels always leak after they have been stored empty for any length of time and it takes at least a week or more to swell the wood to make them tight. Swelling a barrel should be done outdoors, since a great deal of water will leak out in the beginning of the swelling process. Keep filling it up with water until it becomes completely tight. Never start to fill a barrel with wines or ciders if even a single drop is oozing from the barrel, usually from around the rim or chime.

Another "must" is that a barrel should be stored on its side on some kind of rack or stillage. The weight must be supported toward the end of the staves. Resting a barrel directly on a floor or table puts the whole strain of the weight on the center of a stave and the forces on it are then such as to open the seams toward the end of the staves. You may be able to get away with it most of the time, but eventually you will lose a barrel of wine if you insist on thus straining the barrel construction. Barrels are never stored on their ends, since the seal of the head-boards cannot sustain the weight of a full barrel indefinitely.

The ullage problem can be completely solved in our modern age by the use of dry ice: solid carbon dioxide. When you get ready to seal up a barrel for mellowing, drop into the wine or cider a small chunk of dry ice about the size of a walnut, put the bung in place loosely and when the vapor cloud stops streaming from the leaks around the bung, drive it in hard with a mallet.

If you cannot obtain dry ice or want to recreate the older methods more accurately, drop in glass or china eggs to raise the liquid level. Each egg displaces about one quarter cup of liquid. The egg shape is better than a sphere of the same radius, since it has more volume. Geometrically, a cylinder would be even better, but you cannot get a cylinder back out through the bung hole when you are finished with it, so egg shapes are best. Do not use the commonly available alabaster eggs. They dissolve in wines and ciders and will cloud the aged beverage.

The old New England farmers cured their barrels after use by burning sulphur matches in them to be sure they were clean, because in general they did not have running water. If you do have running water, an easy method is to put a hose in the bung hole and let the water run for hours. One straightforward way of knowing when a barrel is clean is to let it sit for a few days and see if it collects fruit flies. If it doesn't, you've done it; if it does, go back and flush it until it doesn't.

One thing that the farmers used to do to "sweeten" a barrel was to rinse the inside surface with rum or brandy after it was swelled tight and before it was filled. It works very well. Barrels that have been used previously to store rum or brandy have always been in great demand for ageing wines and ciders.

A good barrel is an important piece of equipment and can be used for decades if it is properly cared for. One should make a regular habit of oiling the outside with linseed oil after it has been used, cleaned, and dried, and before it is stored to await its next use.

One thing that happens to barrels that have been used for many years is that the bung hole gets to be oblong in shape, longer with the grain and narrower across the grain. When it gets too out-of-round, the bung will no longer fit. Nowadays you can redrill the hole with a tool called a fly cutter and just use a slightly larger bung, but in the old days the farmers used to whittle bungs to fit. I have always had the feeling that the fancy carved or whittled bungs that used to be fashioned in the long winter evenings were lovingly created to honor old faithful barrels whose oblong bungholes no longer fitted any standard bungs.

# Bottling

Since bulk maturing in wood favors oxidation reactions rather than esterification, there will eventually come a time when wine is approaching maturity insofar as oxidation is concerned (which gives it its "wine" taste), but will still be very young with respect to ester formation (which gives it its "fruity" taste). At this point the wine should be bottled to seal the wine effectively from any oxygen and let the ester formation continue without further oxidation. Long before the chemistry of these ageing processes was studied at all, wine makers knew that ageing in wood must be stopped and the beverage bottled. The technique for testing for the proper time has traditionally been to expose a small sample of the wine in a glass overnight. If the wine does not darken, it is ready for bottling.

Recently bottled wine suffers from what used to be called "bottle sickness." A freshly bottled wine tastes flat and uninteresting because of the aeration during the bottling process. This comes from the formation of acetaldehyde. Fortunately, this is only a temporary setback to the wine, which recovers in a few months. It does mean, however, that after bottling, the wine should be aged for another six months at least before use.

Studying, classifying, and collecting colonial bottles is such a specialty for so many people that many books are written on the subject, and magazine articles are appearing all the time on the collecting of bottles of all sorts. It is fun, of course, to serve your recreated old wines and beers in old colonial bottles, but they must be selected with great care. Glass is not a particularly stable material. With age it tends to craze and become brittle. When considering old bottles for refilling, examine the rim of the neck very carefully. If fine cracks are evident anywhere, do not try to use it. The corking process puts a great deal of strain on the neck of a bottle, and it is very likely to shatter if it is not perfect.

Because of the popularity of old bottles, however, a number of manufacturers are making reproductions of particularly noteworthy antique bottles. The glass in them is new and strong, and an air of authenticity can be achieved by putting your recreated wines and ciders in recreated colonial bottles.

# CHAPTER SEVEN

# Hot Mixed Drinks

The early New England farmers were cold a large proportion of the time during the winter months, so it is not surprising that they developed a large number of hot drinks to help banish the chills. New Englanders today who come home in winter in a heated car, drive into a heated garage, and step into an overheated house can never appreciate the glowing satisfaction of a hot mixed drink. But if you do not belong to this womblike culture and do on occasion feel cold, clammy, and basically chilled to the bone, you should experiment with many of these old New England recipes.

Some of them may seem like too much work, some may sound so repelling that you may not even want to try them, and some may be familiar; but in any case try them out. You may find that many will become a regular feature of your winter living. Recipes given here are by no means all you will find in the literature, but they have all been tested and tasted, and they all are good! You should be encouraged to hunt out and try others; if you do, be sure to check in the glossary at the beginning of this book to make sure your cups are cups, how big a wine glass is, and how small a pinch.

Notice also that these concoctions tend to be highly spiced. They were invented long before fermentation or even cleanliness was understood and appreciated. Many of the barrels of beers, ales, ciders, and wines turned out to be almost undrinkable, but with all the time and labor invested in them, the farmers were not about to throw away anything. A heavy dose of spices was a guarantee that even a really unpalatable batch could be rescued and enjoyed on a cold winter evening.

# Abbott's Flip

Break 3 eggs in a quart beer mug and add a teaspoon of sugar for each egg. Stir the eggs and the sugar together; and a jigger of old Medford rum and a jigger of brandy. Beat the eggs briskly while pouring in the liquor. Now fill the mug with beer. The loggerhead (see Glossary) should be red hot, and when the mug is filled, it is thrust into the liquid. The foaming, hissing result is Abbott's flip. (Abbott's Tavern in Holden, Mass., was a stagecoach stop on the route from Keene, N.H., to Worcester, Mass.)

# Ale Flip

Beat 4 eggs and ½ cup of sugar together in a bowl until light. Heat one quart of ale to the boiling point. Skim the foam off the ale and add the foam to the beaten eggs and sugar. Add to the mixture ½ cup of New England rum, ½ teaspoon fresh grated nutmeg, and ½ teaspoon powdered ginger. Add the hot ale, and mix by pouring back and forth from the bowl to a pitcher several times. Serve from the pitcher.

# Ale Posset, 1

To a quart of ale add a slice of buttered toast; let it soak in the ale; grate nutmeg on the bread, also sugar; add one pint of sherry, and serve hot.

# Ale Possett, 2

A much milder, though still warming, posset, is made as follows. Mix a quart of cream with a pint of ale; then beat the yolks of ten eggs and the whites of four. Add the beaten eggs to the cream and ale, sweeten to taste, and flavor with nutmeg. Heat the mixture, stirring constantly. When it becomes thick, but before it boils, remove it from the fire and serve.

# Aleberry

Mix 3 spoonfuls of fine oatmeal with a quart of old ale; boil, strain clear, and sweeten; add juice of one lemon, ¼ grated nutmeg, some powdered ginger, and ½ pint of grape wine. Put a slice of toast on the surface of the liquor.

# Auld Man's Milk

Heat a pint of ale; add, while warming, ¼ ounce of bruised cinnamon, ¼ ounce grated nutmeg, ¼ ounce powdered ginger. Beat the yolks of 2 eggs with a little brown sugar; pour in the ale gradually. When well mixed, add ½ cup of whiskey.

# Bellows-Top

Flip caused to froth abnormally by beating a fresh egg into it.

# Beverige

Heat one quart of hard cider. Add 2 sticks of cinnamon, one teaspoon of whole cloves, and ½ teaspoon grated nutmeg. Bring to boiling point but do not boil. Strain and serve hot.

# Calibogus

Mix ⅓ portion of New England rum with ⅔ portion of spruce beer. Serve hot.

# Cambridge Ale Cup

In 3 pints of water, boil 1 ounce of cloves, 1 ounce of cinnamon, 1 ounce of mace (all bruised together) for one hour. Strain clear and add 3 ounces of powdered sugar, the juice and thin peel of a lemon, 3 pints of ale, and ½ pint of sherry. Heat immediately before serving and add a thin slice of fresh toast with some nutmeg grated on it.

# Colonel Byrd's Nightcap

Put four drops of essence of cloves on four lumps of sugar. Add these to ½ pint of strong ale and a wine glass of brandy. Serve hot and drink when going to bed.

# Early Birds

Heat a quart of ale mixed with a tablespoon of powdered ginger and nutmeg; whisk up with a gill of cold ale, 2 ounces of moist sugar, and 3 eggs. When well frothed up, add the warm ale, by degrees, and a glass of spirits. When this is done, drink without delay.

# Egg Flip

Into a clean saucepan put one quart of good ale; then heat up in a bowl the yolks of 6 fresh eggs, into which grate half a nutmeg, and add ½ pound of moist sugar and a wine glass of gin or whiskey. Beat the eggs, nutmeg, sugar, and liquor thoroughly. As the ale simmers, skim the froth off into the bowl containing the mixture. When the ale nearly boils (do not let it boil), pour it into the mixture, stirring the while. If you use the whites of eggs as well, use only 3 eggs.

# Farmer's Bishop

Stud 5 oranges with cloves; bake for 20 to 25 minutes in a 375°F oven until they begin to ooze. Open one bottle of apple brandy and ½ gallon jug of sweet cider and stand these up to their necks in a large pot of water. Heat but do not boil. Put oranges in the bottom of a bowl; pour the hot brandy over the oranges. Light it and almost immediately douse the flame with the hot cider. Serve in mugs, shaking on top some powdered ginger. Muddle with a cinnamon stick.

# Fit

Fill a pitcher ⅔ full of strong beer. Flavor with sugar, molasses, or dried pumpkin. Fortify with New England rum. Heat with a red hot loggerhead before serving.

# Flip

Fill a quart pewter mug ⅔ full of strong beer. Add sugar to taste; follow it with a gill of rum. Heat a loggerhead red hot and thrust it in.

# Hot Cup

Warm a pint of ale; add one ounce of sugar, one ounce of mixed spices, and a glass of sherry. When nearly boiling, pour it on a round of buttered toast.

# Hot Spiced Ale

Boil one quart of ale; add ½ grated nutmeg; beat up 2 eggs; and mix them with a little cold ale. When ready, add the warm ale; keep stirring to a froth; and add a piece of butter. Serve with dry toast.

# Hot Toddy

Pour one jigger of rum into a hot mug; add one stick of cinnamon and one teaspoon sugar. Fill with piping hot water, and stir with the cinnamon stick.

# Jehu's Nectar

Into a quart pot grate some ginger. Add a wine glass of gin and bitters, then a pint of heated ale. This should be drunk while it is frothing.

# Lamb's Wool

Roast 8 apples, mash them, and add one quart of old ale; press and strain; add ginger and nutmeg (grated). Sweeten to taste, heat, and drink while warm.

# Mulled Cider

Heat, but do not boil, one gallon of cider, either fresh or hard, with 4 sticks of cinnamon and one tablespoon of whole cloves. When hot, dissolve in it one cup of sugar and, if desired, one cup of New England rum. Serve piping hot.

# Negus

Heat a quart of tawny port or medium sherry. Pour into a pitcher. Rub lemon rind on 6 cubes of sugar and add to the wine. Also add 2 or 3 twists of the rind and the juice of one lemon, 2 cups of boiling water. Strain into glasses. Grate nutmeg on top when you serve.

# One-Yard-of-Flannel

A variety of flip. Ale was brought almost to the boil in one pitcher while in another four eggs were beaten up with four ounces of moist sugar, a teaspoonful of grated nutmeg or ginger crushed in a mortar with dried lemon peel, and a quarter of a gill of rum. When the ale was heated the contents of the two pitchers were poured back and forth until the mixture was smooth as cream; then the red hot loggerhead was thrust in.

# Sack-Possett

from the *New York Gazette* (Feb. 13, 1774)

"A Receipt for all young Ladies that are going to be married. To make a

### Sack-Posset

From famed Barbadoes on the Western Main
Fetch sugar half a pound; fetch sack from Spain
A pint; and from the Eastern Indian Coast
Nutmeg, the glory of our Northern toast.
O'er flaming coals together let them let them heat
Till the all-conquering sack dissolves the sweet.
O'er such another fire set eggs, twice ten,
New born from crowing cock and speckled hen;
Stir them with steady hand, and conscience pricking
To see the untimely fate of twenty chicken.
From shining shelf take down your brazen skillet,
A quart of milk from gentle cow will fill it.
When boiled and cooked, put milk and sack to egg,
Unite them firmly like the triple League.
Then covered close, together let them dwell
Till Miss Twice sings: You must not kiss and tell.
Each lad and lass snatch up the murdering spoon,
And fall on fiercely like a starved dragoon.

### Mulled Wine

First, my dear madam, you must take
Nine eggs, which carefully you'll break;
Into a bowl you'll drop the white,
The yolks into another by it.
Let Betsy beat the whites with a switch,
Till they appear quite froth'd and rich.
Another hand the yolks must beat
With sugar, which will make them sweet;
Three or four spoonfuls maybe'll do
Though some, perhaps, would take but two.
Into a skillet next you'll pour
A bottle of good wine, or more;
Put half a pint of water too,
Or it may prove too strong for you:
And while the eggs by two are beating,
The wine and water may be heating;
But when it comes to boiling heat,
The yokes and whites together beat.
With half a pint of water more—
Mixing them well—then gently pour
Into the skillet with the wine,
And stir it briskly all the time.
Then pour it off into a pitcher;
Grate nutmeg in to make it richer;
Then drink it hot, for he's a fool
Who lets such precious liquor cool.

## Scotchem

This concoction is reported to taste like tomato ketchup and usually brought tears to the eyes of the consumer. Having tried it out, I must conclude that tomato ketchup used to taste a lot different than it does now!

To make it, heat to just below the boiling 1 cup applejack and 1 cup water, and blend in 2 teaspoonsful of powdered mustard.

# Stewed Quaker

Hot cider plus as much applejack as desired, with a hot roasted apple floating in it.

# Stone Wall

Heat one quart of hard cider; add one cup of New England rum, one tablespoon dark brown sugar, 4 sticks of cinnamon, 3 whole cloves, ½ teaspoon ground ginger, and a sprinkling of fresh greated nutmeg. Serve piping hot. Sometimes this was made with rum, omitting the brown sugar. One goblet was considered adequate to banish chills and restore normal energy.

# Switchel

"Beverige" strengthened with rum to taste.

# Syllabub

Put a bottle of red or white wine, ale, or cider into a china bowl; sweeten it with sugar and grate in some nutmeg; then hold it under the cow and milk into it till it has a fine froth at the top; strew over it a handful of currants, clean washed and picked, and plumped before the fire. You may make this syllabub without a cow, only use new milk. Heat the milk as hot as milk from the cow and, out of a teapot or anything similar, pour it in, holding your hand very high. The proportions are one quart of hard cider, 4 oz. of sugar, and a liberal grating of nutmeg. Add milk to froth. Beat hard to break up the milk curds.

# Wassail

To one quart of hot ale add ¼ ounce each of grated nutmeg, ginger, and cinnamon; also ½ bottle of sherry, 2 slices of toasted bread, the juice and peel of one lemon, and two well roasted apples. Sweeten to taste.

# Whistle-Belly-Vengeance

Sour beer simmered in a kettle and sweetened with molasses. Crumbs of browned corn bread were added, and it was drunk as hot as could be borne.

# Wine Posset

In one pint of milk boil two or three slices of bread; when soft, remove from the stove, add a little grated nutmeg and one teaspoon sugar; pour into it slowly ½ pint of warm sweet wine. Serve with toasted bread.

# CHAPTER EIGHT

# Cold Mixed Drinks

During the warmer weather cold drinks were as popular in colonial days as they are now, but in general cold drinks were not iced. They were cooled by keeping them in the cellar or in a brook stream. If ice was used, it was not crushed or pounded but used in big blocks which melted slowly and did not quickly dilute the drink.

## Ale Cup

Macerate ¼ ounce of cinnamon, 2 cloves, one allspice, and a little grated nutmeg in a gill of sherry. In two hours strain, press, and put in a jug. Pour in 2 pints of ale and 4 bottles of ginger beer. This is a drink that will make you forget all care.

## Calibogus

Mix ⅓ portion of New England rum with ⅔ portion of spruce beer. Serve cold.

## Cinnamon Tea

To one half pint of fresh milk add stick or ground cinnamon enough to flavor, sugar to taste. Bring to a boil and add brandy as desired. Excellent for diarrhea.

# Cranberry Champagne

Mix 2 quarts of cranberry juice with 2 bottles of champagne and one cup of brandy. Serve over a block of ice in a punch bowl.

# Grog

The cliche that history gets sweeter with the telling is illustrated by a verse popular in the late eighteenth century:

> A mighty bowl on deck he drew,
> And filled it to the brink;
> Such drank the Burford's gallant crew,
> And such the gods shall drink,
> The sacred robe which Vernon wore
> Was drenched within the same;
> And hence his virtues guard our shore,
> And Grog derives its name.

As a matter of history, Admiral Edward Vernon made himself infamous by ordering all rum issued to sailors in the British Navy not to be neat but diluted by at least a factor of two. It was often diluted much more than that, and the term "seven-water-grog" became the contemptuous name for very weak liquor. Vernon was a highly disliked naval officer who was nicknamed "Old Grog" because he always wore a grogram cloak in foul weather and the sailors were quick to name his watered rum after him. He was cashiered out of the Navy in 1746 for behavior unbecoming an officer.

The term "grog" quickly spread to the colonies, but in New England it was used synonymously with "punch" to mean a mixture of rum, spices, fruits, and sugar.

# Mim or Mimbo

Rum, with loaf sugar added to taste.

# Mother-in-Law

Half old and half bitter ale.

# Rhubarb Punch/Vermont Special

The jingle goes:

> One of sour
> And one of sweet
> Two of strong
> And drink it neat.

Verbal tradition says that a Vermont Special is one part lemon or lime juice, one part maple syrup, and two parts New England rum. But the old records tell us to use rhubarb juice, which is surely a much older practice, for the early settlers had no lemons or limes. When you boil up rhubarb in the early spring to make stewed rhubarb or rhubarb sauce, before adding sugar drain off the juice and use that for "one of sour." The taste of the rhubarb is mild, which lets you taste much more of the maple syrup than when you use lemon juice.

# Rumbooze

Beat 4 eggs and add ¼ cup of sugar to 1 quart of ale and 1 pint of white wine. Serve at room temperature.

# Rumfustian

A quart of strong beer, a bottle of sherry, half a pint of gin, the yolks of a dozen eggs, orange peel, nutmegs, spices, and sugar.

# Sillabub, 1

"Fill your Sillabub Pot with Syder (for that is best for a Sillabub) and good store of Sugar and a little Nutmeg, stir it wel together, put in as much thick Cream by two or three spoonfuls at a time, as hard as you can as though you milke it in, then stir it together exceeding softly once about and let it stand for two hours at least."

# Sillabub, 2

The juice of two lemons, half a pound of sugar, mixed in a bowl, a pint of sherry, and grated nutmeg. To this add two quarts of milk.

# Sir Walter Raleigh's Posset

Take ½ pint of dry sherry or white wine and ½ pint of ale. Add a quart of boiled cream and strain through a tammy (see Glossary). This was a favorite remedy for colds.

# Splitting Headache

Put into ¼ pint of rum, ½ dozen crushed cloves, and a little cinnamon, ginger, and nutmeg; strain in an hour, with pressure. Add an equal quantity of lime juice and 2 quarts of ale.

# Tea Punch

Peel 12 lemons in thin strips and place them in a large bowl. Pour a quart of strong hot tea over the peels, add 2 cups of sugar, and stir until dissolved. Add the juice of the 12 lemons and stir in 2 quarts of New England rum, one cup of brandy, and a quart of cold water. Allow the mixture to sit at room temperature for at least two hours before drinking. If you want to chill it, add a block of ice.

# Further Reading

Having come to the end of this book, you should be motivated to start not only to make the drinks for yourself but also to do further research into early American wines, beers, and ciders. Here is a brief list of books.

Amerine, M. A.; Berg, H. W.; Cruess, W. V. *The Technology of Wine Making*, 3rd ed. (Avi Publishing Co., Westport, Conn., 1972), 802 pp. An up-to-date advanced textbook on enology by members of the faculty of the University of California at Davis.

Baron, Stanley. *Brewed in America: A History of Beer and Ale in the United States* (Little Brown and Co., Boston, 1962), 424 pp. A history of beer making from the first settlers through Prohibition.

Brown, John Hull. *Early American Beverages* (Bonanza Books, New York, 1966), 171 pp. Has extensive lists of recipes for mixed drinks, cordials, and medicinal beverages.

Clark, Charles E. *The Eastern Frontier: The Settlement of Northern New England, 1610–1763* (Alfred A. Knopf, New York, 1970), 419 pp. A detailed study of the life of common people in early New England.

*The Closet of Sir Kenelme Digbie Opened, Whereby is Discovered Several ways of making of Metheglin, Sider, Cherry-Wine, &c.* (H. Brome, London, 1669), 312 pp. Hundreds of recipes. The book was reproduced by Mallinckrodt Chemical Works in 1967.

Crahan, Marcus Esketh. *Early American Inebrietatis* (The Zamorano Club, Los Angeles, 1964), 62 pp. A history of overdrinking from colonial times through the first quarter of the nineteenth century.

Duncan, Peter; Acton, Bryan. *Progressive Winemaking* (The Amateur Winemaker, Andover, England, 1970), 425 pp. An introductory textbook of modern wine making, with careful explanations of the techniques and chemistry.

Fuller, Andrew S. *The Grape Culturist: A Treatise on the Cultivation of the Native Grape* (Davies & Kent, New York, 1865), 262 pp. Detailed instructions on early East Coast grapevine management.

*Mackenzie's Five Thousand Receipts, Constituting a Complete Practical Library relative to Bees . . . Brewing . . . Distillation . . . Trees of all kinds . . . Wines &c.&c.&c.* (James Kay, Philadelphia, 1829), 456 pp. Typical of eighteenth and nineteenth century recipe books.

Nearing, Helen and Scott. *The Maple Sugar Book* (Schocken Books, New York, 1970), 273 pp. Discusses historical as well as modern methods of collecting and using maple tree sap.

Noling, A. W. *Beverage Literature: A Bibliography* (The Scarecrow Press, Inc., Metuchen, New Jersey, 1971), 865 pp. A very extensive bibliography, with full cross-references and indexes.

Orton, Vrest. *The American Cider Book: The Story of America's Natural Beverage* (The Noonday Press, New York, 1973), 136 pp. Gives a history of cider and includes 34 pages of recipes, many of them old.

Phaff, H. J.; Miller, M. W.; Mrak, E. M. *The Life of Yeasts* (Harvard U. Press, Cambridge, Mass., 1968), 186 pp. Discusses their nature, activity, ecology, and relation to mankind.

Richardson, John. *The Philosophical Principles of the Science of Brewing* (Hull, England, 1798), 458 pp. Early advocate of the use of a thermometer and saccharometer in beer making.

# Index